*"...Therefore if the Son makes you free,
you shall be free indeed..."*

–JESUS (John 8:36)

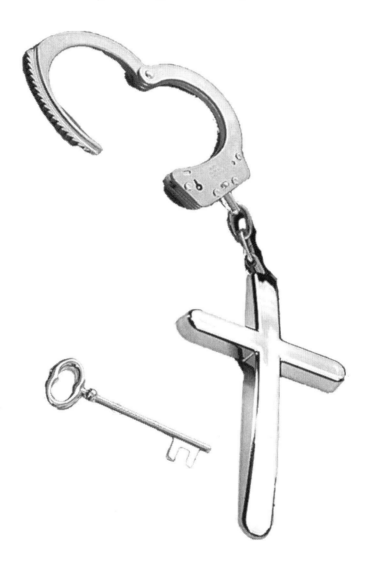

From a Convict to a Convert
By: Michael Berrian Jr., © 2017

Published by: *iRepDaKING!*
iRepDaKING.com

ISBN-13: 978-0692577257
ISBN-10: 0692577254

Book cover design by:
Frank Cage | CAGE DESIGN (cage-design.com)

Caterpillar, cocoon, and butterfly illustrations by:
William Hogan | BASSIC ARTS (w.hogan97.wh@gmail.com)

This book recounts events in the life of Michael Berrian Jr. according to the author's recollection and perspective. While all the stories are true, some names and identifying details have been changed to protect the privacy of those involved.

iRepDaKING!

Glorifying JESUS Christ
(through books, music, and apparel)

iRepDaKING.com

DEDICATION

*To: **Amiracle, Mikayla, and Michael (III)**, I prayed for children and God was faithful to answer my prayer by giving me you. As you very well know, it was **JESUS** Christ that found me when I was lost and showed me that I needed Him. Out of all the wrong I did, He still loved me and wanted me. He forgave me of my sins and opened my eyes to His truth. He gave me His Spirit and filled my heart with His Word. He has not and never will leave me and it is my most earnest prayer that He does all of the above for you. Be not wise in your own eyes, love and fear God. Learn from all the bad choices I made in life. God has a plan and purpose for your lives. Don't waste your lives pursuing vain things, but "pursue peace with everyone, and holiness, without which no one will see the Lord" (**Hebrews 12:14**). Give your all to God. **JESUS** Christ is the only way to the Father (God) and the only way into Heaven. Love, trust, obey, and follow Him with your whole heart. Remember, He desires to have a relationship with you. I pray that just as a sponge soaks up water, may your hearts soak up His words found in the Holy Bible. May He be glorified in your lives.* **I love you forever!**

-Your Father

*To: **King Jr. and Luke Jr.**, the message above applies to you as well. Be better than me and your fathers were. Be great! Follow **JESUS** and His teachings. God wants a relationship with you and has a plan for your lives, surrender to His will. I love you. –**Your "God Father"***

THANK YOU

To my wife, Shandale: Thank you for your encouragement and patience through the process of me writing this book and also for making me aware of all the many edits that would be needed. You gave me the extra push when I needed it. You are so wonderful and such a blessing to my life. You are the one for me and I want to spend my whole life with you. You are forever my lady!

To my mother, Lennie: Thank you for every letter you took the time to write me, for every money order you sacrificed to send me, for all the prayers you prayed and asked others to pray on my behalf, for every time you visited me, and for believing in me when I didn't believe in myself. Your support really meant a lot while I was incarcerated. So many parents give up on their children, but thank you for never giving up on me and for trusting in God for my deliverance from living in darkness (sin) and prison. For every time you encouraged me, for every seed you sowed verbally and financially into my life, thank you! Your love for me is the most genuine. You are a true treasure and the best mother I could ever ask for! I'm deeply sorry for all the disrespect, trouble, and pain I caused you. I thank God I am able to make you proud now.

To my aunt, Linda: You really proved your love for me while I was incarcerated and I appreciate you so much. Thank you for writing me letters, visiting me, and all the other things you've done. It meant so much!

◀ SPECIAL THANKS ▶

To my editors, Shandale Berrian, Kellie Sullivan, Kimberlee Hilliard, Edward Lewis, Deborah Scales, Donta Thorpe, Chad Green, and Carolyn Rainey: Thank you for taking the time out of your busy schedules to proofread and make the necessary edits to *"From a Convict to a Convert"*. Your help was a Godsend! Thank you so much for undergirding me during this tedious process and helping me make it the best it could possibly be.

PROLOGUE

A son, a brother, and a friend...

*God has truly done and is doing a marvelous work in you. The saving of your soul, the regeneration of your spirit, and the renewing of your mind are evident by your walk of faith. You've distinguished yourself as a man who not only wants to enter the gates, but go beyond the court into the holy of holies. I'm especially proud of you for being a beacon of light and an inspiration to me. Like you were, I was once lost, wounded, broken, and reckless. Also, like yours, my life once consisted of many trials and dark days. God brought me through twenty-five years of imprisonment in the federal prison system and set me free! He kept us here! His love captured us! He opened our eyes! He has written our names in His book of Life and has given us His Word to hold dear. It encourages me that He wanted my spirit to embrace your spirit because you have set the atmosphere. Your walk of faith demonstrates that you've accepted the prophetic call and charge to carry the Gospel of **JESUS** Christ, promote the Kingdom of God, and be used for His glory. I appreciate you, because through a close walk with you God has opened the eyes of my understanding that we've been identified for a great purpose in the Kingdom of God. For this purpose we were born. Therefore, let's go forth my son, my brother, and my friend in the power and authority we have in our Lord and Savior **JESUS** Christ.*

-**Edward B. Lewis**

From a Convict to a Convert

TABLE OF CONTENTS

PART 1: THE CATERPILLAR

PART 2: THE COCOON

PART 3: THE BUTTERFLY

INTRODUCTION

MY NAME IS MICHAEL BERRIAN JR., but you can call me Mike. My eyes are open now and I can clearly see as I travel on this straight and narrow road that ends in life and peace. It hasn't always been this way in my life, I haven't always been on this road. As far back as I can remember I was living in the dark, blind to the truth, and traveling full speed ahead down the broad and wide road that ends in destruction.

I was selling crack cocaine, smoking weed, drinking alcohol, fornicating (having pre-marital sex), masturbating, robbing, stealing, cursing, fighting, lying, disrespectful (to my parents and other adults), selfish, gang-affiliated, running from God and in love with the world and its ways. It's hard to believe that in the midst of all of this a loving God had His mind on me. **JESUS** Christ pursued me until He captured me. He opened my eyes and saved me from a life of bondage and sin. He delivered me. He truly sets the captives free, I am proof.

My life is much like that of a butterfly. A butterfly isn't born a butterfly, it's born a caterpillar. There's a process (a transformation, a conformation) called metamorphosis that a caterpillar must go through in order to become what it is destined to be. I was a caterpillar that made a lot of bad decisions which led to my cocoon, prison. Take a walk with me and see how I was transformed *"From a Convict to a Convert"* by the grace and mercy of God. I didn't choose Him, He chose me **(John 15:16)**...

May God be glorified through this book!!!
He deserves the praise and worship, not me.
All that I am today is because of who He is...

PART 1:

THE CATERPILLAR

1

Product of My Environment

◀ BACK HOME ▶

My Neighborhood

Winter, 2002... Riding on a Greyhound bus, heading back home...

I HAD JUST TURNED SIXTEEN years old a few weeks ago on January 31st, 2002. I was coming back home from *Youth Challenge Academy*, a military school located at Fort Stewart (an army base) in Hinesville, GA. My mother, Lennie, had sent me off to *Youth Challenge Academy* because she wanted me to do something better with my life than just waste it. She wanted to keep me alive and help me accomplish something in life because at that time in my life I was on a downward spiral headed towards destruction.

The school was a "six-month" program and I could've completed it, received a diploma, and really made something of myself. My mother would've been so proud of me. I wish I could tell you that's how it ended, but disappointingly I was expelled from *Youth Challenge Academy* within about a month of being there. I continuously stayed in trouble. Honestly, I purposely made it my business to get kicked out of the school because I truly didn't want to be there; therefore I acted out. I couldn't take the discipline, waking up early, excessive exercising, being told what to do, and when to do it, amongst other things. I was missing my family, friends, and neighborhood. I didn't understand the privilege it was to even be accepted into a school like this and the advantages it would allow me to have in life. I was insubordinate and disobedient to the ones in charge over me until I found myself on a Greyhound bus heading back to Macon, GA.

At that time, we were living on Third Ave. in

Pleasant Hill, the neighborhood I was r.
my arrival back home, I found out that n
started dating a guy named Rich. I didn't
first but it felt like I knew him or had see
After being home awhile I found out why ~~ likely
had that feeling, Rich was on drugs. Eventually a great
deal of problems came from their being together. They
were *"unequally yoked" (according to **2nd Corinthians
6:14)**;* my mother was a Christian and not living the
same lifestyle as her new boyfriend. Nonetheless, she
was compromising in her walk with God by being with
him.

I didn't really want to go back to the old lifestyle
that I left when I went to military school, but before I
knew it I was back on the block selling drugs, smoking
weed, and doing the same old thing with the same old
crew that only influenced me in the same old way,
negatively. My mother still took me to church, but I
wasn't interested any more. I was in love with the
"world" (the ways of the world, the system).

My mother raised me and my younger brother,
Brandon, on her own and tried to steer us in the right
direction. She was a single parent with no consistent
support from our dads at that time. Looking back at
that time, I didn't have a good, positive "father figure" in
my life. All the men that I knew or wanted to be like
were on the wrong path in life. They were either drug
dealers, gang bangers, womanizers, etc. I hadn't seen
my dad, Michael (Sr.), in a while, I'm not sure what he
was into or where he was at that time. I really put my
mother through a lot of hurt and pain, often

_specting her, disobeying her, and putting her life in anger as well as my younger brother. At that time in my life, I didn't know how to be a good role model to him.

Going home from school one day, some friends and I went up onto the railroad track which was on a big hill down the street from the school we attended. As vehicles passed by, we began to throw large rocks at them. We were hiding behind the tall trees so that no one could clearly see us. We used the pathway on the other side of the train tracks to escape. We ran after hearing a loud clashing noise and realizing that we had possibly damaged a vehicle. I ended up in police custody that day and although I did deserve it, I didn't receive any jail time. My mother had to come pick me up from the police precinct and I know she wasn't happy.

On another occasion I asked my mother about getting a tattoo and she told me not to get one, but I still came home with *"P-Hill"* tattooed on my arm anyway. I was a rebel and though she tried, I was dead set in my ways to do what I wanted to do. I didn't realize that the downward spiral I was on was going to end with me being in jail or hell.

◄ KING AND LUKE ►

I had two close friends who were more like brothers to me, their names were King and Luke. King was fourteen, Luke was fifteen, and I was sixteen. King was originally from up north near New York but had moved to Georgia with his family when he was much younger and Luke was from the Westside of Macon. I met King first and we became close friends really quick. He was twelve at that time and I was fourteen. I became like one of his family members, I was at his house all the time. He was like a comedian always cracking jokes. He kept everyone laughing. He loved to rap and he did it all the time. He was very good at it.

Shortly after meeting King, we met and became close friends with Luke. He had moved in with his dad who lived nearby the Pleasant Hill area. Since we all lived near each other, we hung out together most days. It was very rare not to see us together. This was my crew, my brothers, and my family. I loved them and would do almost anything for them. Fighting against one of us was like fighting against all of us. We were all lost like sheep without a shepherd, young and reckless. We did whatever we wanted to do. We lived our lives with no accountability to no one, not God nor our parents.

◄ MERCY IN THE TRAP HOUSE ►

About two months or so before my mother sent me off to *Youth Challenge Academy*, I was caught up in a situation where I could've been murdered had not the grace of God been present with me at that very moment.

On that day, my friend Dae-Dae and I skipped school and caught the *(Macon Transit Authority)* bus to the Southside of Macon. We had made plans to go over some girls' house who was also not going to school that day. We got off the bus on Houston Ave. and called them from a pay phone nearby and found out that their mother didn't go to work that day either. Our plans were spoiled.

After a short while, we got on the bus again and headed back to Pleasant Hill. After making it back to our side of town, we walked to one of the *"trap houses" (a house where drugs are sold, also called "trap" for short)* in our neighborhood. We were there playing a video game when all of a sudden a guy named Black came into the room that we were in and began to point a gun (22 revolver) at us and started pulling the trigger, but no bullets came out of the gun. At that time, I believe he was high, drunk, or both because no one in their right mind would play with a gun like that. We supposed to have been friends so I didn't know what was going on or why he was doing this to us. We shouted at him, "Man, stop playing!" and he replied, "I'll do it for real!" Then, we saw him reach into his pocket, open the cylinder, put one bullet into a chamber of the revolver, and close it. He then began to point the gun at us again. We both jumped up and ran into the kitchen area of the very small apartment we were in. Dae-Dae ran to the left side of the kitchen and I ran to the right side of the kitchen on the side of the refrigerator. Black came into the kitchen and after finding me he put the gun to the left side of my head. I was in a corner with nowhere to run.

At that moment, I didn't understand the severity of what I was facing. You hear people talk about your life flashing before your eyes at moments like this. I don't remember if I saw my life flash or not, but one thing I do remember is that I was afraid and felt helpless. I would've never thought in a million years that this is how my life would end... murdered in a "trap house" from a gunshot wound to the head at the tender age of fifteen.

What happens after you die? Does everybody end up in Heaven where God is? I'd heard about Heaven, Hell, JESUS, and Satan (the devil) often and at that time in my life I think I really believed that God was real. I believed I was a Christian. I went church and all that, I said my prayers before I went to bed some nights, and I could even quote Psalms 23 and "The Lord's Prayer" (Matthew 6:9-13) in its entirety. However, I was not who I thought I was and dying without JESUS in my life wasn't even on my mind or the fact that if I died in my sins I would've ended up in a real, burning Hell. I don't believe I'd even really thought about dying much at that time in my life. I was young and had a long life ahead of me, right?

Then it happened, 'Click!' was all that I heard as Black pulled the trigger, but no bullet came out of the gun. Before he pulled the trigger, I remember calling on the name of JESUS from within my heart while he had the gun pointed at my head. Although I didn't say it out loud nor was I living for Him, I believe with all my heart that JESUS heard me and had mercy on me that day and kept me from being murdered and I give Him the glory for that; Hallelujah!

Dae-Dae ran to the front door in an attempt to

escape but wasn't allowed to because someone was blocking the door. He turned around with his back to the door and held his hands in the air and said to Black, "You already did me!" Black pointed the gun at my friend and after a few moments he pulled the trigger. 'Boom!' The bullet came out and scraped the area underneath his chin and went into his neck. At first I didn't see anything happening, Dae-Dae was still standing and Black had dropped the gun on the floor after firing the shot. After a few moments, blood began to gush out of his neck. Eventually he was rushed to the hospital and treated for the gun-shot wound of which he survived. He was only fourteen at that time and I know it was only by God's grace and mercy that he didn't die. Black was never arrested for this incident. A newspaper article came out shortly after that day about the incident and it stated that we were playing "Russian Roulette", but that was far from the truth. When my mother found out what had taken place in the "trap", she made all of us (herself, my brother, and I) sleep on the floor in fear that someone would think that I had "snitched" (told the police what happened) and come to shoot up our house. That's one of the top reasons she sent me to *Youth Challenge Academy*.

> *"Eyes closed, blinded, I couldn't see...*
> *I was a young teen on the block selling weed...*
> *then I graduated on up to crack cocaine...*
> *before I knew it I was trapped in the "trap game"...*
> *running the streets at all times of the night...*
> *disrespecting my mama, I knew I wasn't right...*
> *but I was being used, by Satan I was being fooled..*

letting my pants sag thinking I was being cool...
but I was being rude, I should've been in school...
but I was fifteen in the "trap" with my crew...
then one day there was a gun put to my head...
and the trigger pulled, I should've been dead..."

◄ MAKING MONEY ►

I was allowed to work at the *Booker T. Washington Community Center* the previous summer (2001) through *Macon Workforce Development.* They hired teenagers to work at various places through the summer time. I believe this was my first "real" job, however a couple of years before that I was making money other ways. An older guy named Mr. Benton allowed me to do some yard work with him from time to time and he would pay me cash. I also walked and picked up aluminum cans off the streets (and out of yards and recycle bins that didn't belong to me) for my Uncle Earnest who paid me cash as well. With *Macon Workforce Development,* I was paid by check and it came with a check stub. The *Booker T. Washington Community Center* was located on the bottom side of Pleasant Hill and every summer they had a program. To me it was like a daycare center minus the little babies. The age limits ranged from about five years old to eighteen years old. I attended the center myself when I was much younger, but now I was on the other side of things. While working there I had a lot of fun. The job ended when summer break was over and it was time to go back to school.

After several months of being in school I began

to skip classes and be more involved in the street life. I began to make money illegally. I remember the first time I ever touched crack cocaine. I had gotten a "deal" (dope for a discounted price) from Dope Boy. He allowed me to buy two crack cocaine rocks (worth $20) from him for $15. I could make a $5 profit off of it. From there, I could get another "deal" from him or someone else and buy three rocks (worth $30) for $20. I was only fifteen and wanted to be down with the crowd so much that the little profit I would be making was worth it to me at that time, I was just having fun. So there I was on the block selling drugs as a young teenager. I wasn't sure of what I was doing, but I wanted to fit in with everything that was going on around me. My mother knew Dope Boy and had heard that he'd allowed me to buy drugs from him to sell and she wasn't happy at all. She knew all about drug dealing because she was on drugs and sold drugs herself at a time in her life. She didn't want me to be involved with that kind of lifestyle.

◄ TRYING TO COME UP ►

We were always trying to "come up" (make a lot of money). One day a guy named Pédro (pronounced Pay-dro) offered to give me some dope upfront to sell and bring him back a percentage of it and keep the rest for myself. There were many advantages that came along with the offer and I quickly agreed to do it. This was the first time someone had ever offered to give me something for nothing upfront and pay them back later.

Pédro wanted to see me "come up". I remember him giving me "dime rocks" (crack cocaine, cut up and shaped like squares, worth $10 a piece) to sell for him, out of it I was supposed to bring him back his cut and then he would give me more, that was the deal. Thinking back on this moment, that was not a lot of money to be risking my life for, but I don't believe I was thinking about any of that at that time. I was just happy to have a supplier and a little money in my pockets. It felt good to be able to hustle in the midst of the other drug dealers and be accepted. At any time, I had a steady supply of dope at my fingertips that I could access. All I had to do is make sure that I brought him back his cut on every "pack" (dope package) he gave me and I would always be supplied. Although I had agreed to the offer, I still didn't understand how to properly take advantage of the opportunity that he offered me. I was struggling trying to make money before Pédro came and offered to be my "plug" (drug supplier) and I found myself still struggling afterward. I wasted a lot of my profit on frivolous things, mostly marijuana to smoke. I should've saved enough money up to buy my own dope so that I could pocket 100% of the profit.

When King heard about the opportunity I had received, he went to Pédro and they made an agreement among themselves. So Pédro became both of our supplier. Luke had his own "plug" named Gold Mouth, he dated Luke's cousin. Although we had money and dope flowing smoothly through our hands, we stayed below average monetarily. Being young in the "game" (drug distribution), we were not properly taking advantage of the money we were making. We would mostly sell crack cocaine and then go buy marijuana to smoke with most of our money. We were wasting our lives. To us, going to the skating rink was a highlight of the week. At that time going to the skating rink was like adults going to the club, we had fun. We would spend money doing that on the weekends. There was a lot more for us to do there than skate and that's what really motivated us to go Saturday after Saturday. We went for the girls! There was a time to skate then there was a time to dance. The guys would pick different girls or vice versa to dance with song after song. Lust would fill my heart and I would want to do more than just dance with them. I was always on the hunt for a girl that I could have sex with, honestly, that's all I wanted from them at that time in my life. I was so selfish. Although I did have a few girlfriends from time to time, I was too busy living "the street life" to pursue a real relationship with them. Therefore, I just slept around from female to female, I wasn't committed to none of them.

We thought we had it made and were making progress but we were hustling backwards. We had solid "plugs", but our lack of worldly wisdom kept us running in circles like a dog chasing its tail. We risked our lives on the block selling drugs but really had nothing to show for it. We were living in darkness and blind to the light. We were content with the wicked lifestyle we were living and saw no need for change.

"I'm coming to you str8 from the heart of Georgia, Macon...
I grew up on the topside of Pleasant Hill paper chasing...
I wanted to be like the big homies around...
I wanted to be sitting twenty-four inches off of the ground...
so I had to get it by any means...
selling crack, breaking in houses, armed robbery...
smoked out, weed head, soon I will be dead...
on the highway to Hell breaking laws, speeding...
sexing pre-marital so many times...
so much lust in my eyes I could've went blind...
naked images, limitless filthy thoughts...
multiple sex partners had me feeling like a boss...
posted on the block all night with that all white...
crack in my fist balled tight feeling alright..."

The Block

On the corner of Penn Ave. and Mutual Ave. was one of the spots in Pleasant Hill where a lot of the action took place and we were right in the middle of it. King lived on that same corner and drugs were being sold right out of his front yard. So many people in the area had their hands in the "game" one way or another, whether selling drugs or smoking drugs. My friends and I took turns serving the "customers" (drug addicts). I had been selling dope for a while at that time. I still had no clue what I was really doing nor did I realize the many dangers that I put myself in the midst of every time I decided to sell drugs.

One night we were out on the block and a man named Ranger pulled up in a truck and asked to buy drugs. It was King's turn to serve so he went out to the truck to see what the "customer" wanted. After King gave Ranger the two dime rocks that he came for, he looked at the money he had received from him and noticed that he had been tricked. What supposed to have been a $20 bill was actually a $1 bill tightly balled up. At that instance King reached in the truck, I'm guessing in attempt to get his dope back. Ranger smashed on the gas petal and sped off with King still hanging onto the truck. After being dragged about twenty feet or so away, King fell from the truck and landed on the concrete street while Ranger continued to drive fast up Mutual Ave. Blood was coming from King's head while he laid there, but he was still alive. Everybody was shocked and angry at what had just taken place. He was taken to the hospital a short while after that.

He returned to the block with a hospital gown on and the first thing he wanted to do was smoke a blunt of weed. He had a big afro, but now there was a patch of his hair missing because he had to receive a few stitches from the incident. It could have been much worse. Ranger didn't even stop at the stop sign; if there had been another car coming, it would have ran right into him and King would've been affected by that as well. He could've died at the tender age of fourteen from that fall, and for what? $20? Two dime rocks? In the midst of all that happening, King lost his "pack" that contained about six rocks in it. After Pédro found out what had taken place, he stopped supplying us with drugs because he didn't want no one else to get hurt or even killed on his account.

This is only one of many risks that a person who decides to sell drugs takes when they are on the block living that life. Some people addicted to drugs will do almost anything to get it, including hurting or even killing someone for it. I personally had an encounter where an older lady offered to have a sexual encounter with me for drugs. I was only sixteen years old at that time sexually involved with a lady that had to at least be in her mid-thirties. At any given time, we could easily rent a car from a "customer" for a few hours to even days at a time for drugs. Some "customers" would steal items and bring it to the block and attempt to sell it for drugs, sometimes they would succeed. Like I said before, people will do almost anything to satisfy their hunger for drugs. With drug dealers included, they will argue, fight, plot against one another and even commit murder over money, drugs, or status. Envy and jealousy can motivate anyone to take a life if they want what you have or the position you got bad enough. Almost everybody wants power, money, and respect. They want the number one spot, but lust and greed only leads to destruction. What kind of life is it when you have to live constantly looking over your shoulders because so many people (drug addicts, other drug dealers, robbers, and the police) are out to take you down? When I look back and think about the numerous amount of people that I know that sold drugs, I don't see any good outcome from most of their lives. Selling drugs can lead to hard time behind prison bars, faces on t-shirts, hurt, pain, and emptiness, unless they stop selling them. But even then you still risk the chance of being caught up on a conspiracy charge or something even worse because of people thinking you made enough money to get out the "game". Someone could come and attempt to take what you have (or what they think you have) by force.

You may ask drug dealers why they sell drugs and they may say that they do it to provide for their family. That's not the full truth. The bottom line is they are in love with the fast money and the lifestyle that selling drugs allow them to live. The real truth is they are addicts as well. They are addicted to the money and the lifestyle just as their "clientele" (customers) are addicted to the drugs. When you think about it, in the midst of them 'providing for their family' they are destroying other families at the same time.

"*Let me take you to my hood Pleasant Hill homie...*
where a lot of my people got killed homie...
Mutual Ave., I used to crack deal on it...
King got his head busted, blood spilled on it...
only by the grace of God He did live homie...
I pray you give your life to Christ little homie...
anyway, back to the block...
posted up all night, matchbox full of rocks...
risking my life to the jack boys...
to the addicts,, to the cops and other trap stars..."

2

Following the Crowd

FROM THIRD AVE., WE MOVED down the street into another house on Empire Ave. It was right across the street from my grandmother's house and around the corner from *L.H. Williams*, the elementary school I went to when I was younger. My mother ended up marrying Rich and I was no longer attending school, I was officially a "high school drop-out". Before I had dropped out of school completely, I had gone to *Miller Middle School, Central High School, Westside High School, and the Bibb County Alternative School.* When I was in the eighth grade, I was expelled from *Miller Middle School* and sent to the *Bibb County Alternative School* for their "Eighteen-Week" program. *Miller Middle School* only allowed students to have about fifteen disciplinary write ups before they expelled them. Before I was finally kicked out, I had received over fifty write ups. They tried giving me chance after chance, but I kept messing up. Most of the times, I abused the grace given to me time after time.

After serving eighteen weeks in the Alternative School, I was promoted to the ninth grade and was allowed to enter back into the public school system.

While at *Central High School*, I began to skip school and smoke weed more frequently. I also became more affiliated with a gang. I wanted to be recognized and respected in my neighborhood and at school. I wanted to be "that guy". I wanted everyone to know who I was. I wanted to be a leader, but all I was becoming was a follower. All of these desires were leading me to destruction, but I didn't know it. So, I dove in head first into the "pool of the world".

I flunked my first year of ninth grade and was held back. In my second year of the ninth grade, I was eventually expelled from *Central High School* and sent back to the *Bibb County Alternative School* for another eighteen weeks. I believe I was very smart, but I couldn't get pass the negative influences of the world around me nor the ever increasing evil desires in my heart.

◄ HAVE YOU SEEN MY DAD? ►

At that time, I began to dislike my dad as a teenager for not being in my life. Before my parents met each other, they were previously married, but they never married each other. When my dad met my mother, he was still legally married. After I was born, their relationship ended a couple years later. For a short while when I was much younger, I slightly remember living with my dad. For the majority of my life I had lived with my mother and hadn't seen my dad in a very long time. As I was growing up, my parents both had problems in their lives that I didn't understand.

When I was a little boy, my uncle said whenever

I came around I asked him, "Have you seen my dad?" It didn't really matter to me 'the reason why' he wasn't there in my life, but it only mattered that he wasn't there. I did get chances to see him from time to time at family gatherings during the holiday seasons such as Thanksgiving and Christmas. It felt good to be in the same atmosphere that he was in. When I was younger, I remember him buying me a train set for my birthday and I treasured it.

When I was about fifteen years old, I remember seeing him one day in my neighborhood at a *"boot leg"* *(a house where alcohol, cigars, cigarettes, etc. is sold, similar to a "trap house", but minus the drugs)*. At that time, I don't believe I had seen him in a long while. King and I were together and we were too young to buy cigars from the other stores around the neighborhood. When we wanted to smoke a blunt, we only had two choices and one was ask an adult to buy us a cigar from a store or go to a "boot leg" and get one ourselves. King stood on the front porch as I walked inside the "boot leg" to purchase a cigar. At first, I wasn't paying attention to my surroundings. Then I looked to my left and saw my dad sitting on the sofa with a look of amazement on his face. I can imagine he was thinking in his head, *"I know my son didn't just come in here and ask to buy a cigar!"* Afterwards, my dad followed me on the porch and tried his best to talk us out of smoking and the way that we were living our lives. His words held no weight because of his absence in my everyday life; I didn't want to hear anything he had to say about the way I was living my life. Why should I? Although he was telling us not to smoke, he had cigarettes and a can of beer himself.

My dad was gifted and talented in many ways, but he was mostly known as a carpenter. The devil was stealing his life away through an addiction to alcohol and other things that held him captive and disallowed him from being in my life (**John 10:10**). As his son, I wanted him to see me as someone significant, but the devil was attempting to kill two birds with one stone. The devil desired to destroy both of our lives. His advice went in one ear and out the other because at that moment the only things on my mind were money, sex, and drugs.

◄ FIRST COUNT (ARMED ROBBERY) ►

King, Luke, and I were out walking around the Pleasant Hill area late one night scheming and plotting on how we would get some money. We walked for what seemed like hours. In the midst of walking we came together and made a vow that we would not go home until we had robbed someone. Now looking back at that moment I understand why Solomon (King David's son) said to not let others entice you to do wrong (**Proverbs 1:8-19**). I understand now that God made me a leader. Since I didn't know who I was, I settled for following everyone else around me because I was so easily influenced. I could've said, "No, we don't need to do this". If I had spoken up, I really believe I could've persuaded my two friends not to do it as well. Being the oldest of us three, you would think that I was the one with the most influence in the group, but I wasn't. I believe it would be safe for me to say that King, the youngest among us, was actually the most influential one. He was very persuasive and had a way with words that would make you jump on board with almost everything he was saying, but he was also a follower just as the rest of us. It wasn't his fault that we were out looking for someone to rob that night; we all encouraged and enticed one another to do negative things all the time. We were all being followers. We all wanted to be *"down" (accepted; we all wanted to fit in)*. We all wanted to be what we thought was "Gangster". No one wanted to be considered the one that was always scared. This is one of the reasons we were out so late because neither one of us wanted to break the vow we had made together. So as vowed, we did not go home until we robbed someone.

We ended up walking onto the grounds of an apartment complex. We walked down a hill and found a spot to wait on some random person to stumble across our path so that we could rob him or her. After waiting a while, someone finally came down the hill in a vehicle and parked. As soon as the person got out of the vehicle, we pounced on them like three hungry young lions on a gazelle. Luke pointed the gun at the victim as we all screamed statements and demanded the individual to "Give us the money!" Immediately the victim gave us a wallet and we ran back up the hill. While running up the hill, Luke tossed the gun into some bushes. We all went home because the vow we had made *"to not go home until we robbed someone"* had been accomplished. There wasn't much money in the wallet we stole.

While the victim was on the phone with the police reporting the robbery, he revealed to them that he had a gun in a holster under his arm in the midst of being robbed by us. The victim told the police the only reason he didn't shoot us (or at least at us) was because he knew that we were young. God had mercy on us! He could've fired a few shots in the crowd as we ran up the hill. One or all of us could've been shot or possibly killed. It could've been me! But God, who is rich in mercy, gave me yet another chance at life to live, but I didn't deserve or appreciate it.

I have learned that being a follower will put you into positions to do things that you know are wrong. Being a follower will have you doing things that you don't even want to do, but for the sake of pleasing others you will do it anyway. According to **JESUS** in **Matthew 7:13-14**, the *"broad and wide road"* that leads to destruction is very crowded. If you knew that Hell was at the end of the road you were traveling, would you still continue to travel in that direction? Would you still follow the crowd if they were going that way? **JESUS** also mentioned another road that only a few would find, the *"straight and narrow road"*. He said that this road leads to life and peace. God has set before us life and death to choose, He desires that we choose life and live **(Deuteronomy 30:19)**.

Proverbs 1:8-19 (NKJV) **"My son, hear the instruction of your father, and do not forsake the law of your mother;**

For they will be a graceful ornament on your head, and chains about your neck. My son, if sinners entice you, Do not consent. If they say, "Come with us, Let us lie in wait to shed blood; Let us lurk secretly for the innocent without cause; Let us swallow them alive like Sheol (the grave, the place of the dead), and whole, like those who go down to the pit (of death); We shall find all kinds of precious possessions, We shall fill our houses with spoil; Cast in your lot among us, Let us all have one purse"— My son, do not walk in the way with them, Keep your foot from their path; For their feet run to evil, And they make haste to shed blood. Surely, in vain the net is spread in the sight of any bird; But they lie in wait for their own blood, They lurk secretly for their own lives. So are the ways of everyone who is greedy for gain; it takes away the life of its owners..."

◄ FULL REBELLION ►

My mother was a Christian and she always worried about my lifestyle. She worked very hard to take care of us. She desired to keep us in the church and teach us how to live right the way the best she knew how. Her eyes were opened to **JESUS** Christ in 1991, He changed her life and delivered her from a crack cocaine addiction of three and a half years.

Before she got "saved" (became a Christian; born again) she prayed and asked God for a child one day as she looked into the wooded area behind the home that my dad and her were living in. I believe her being able to bear me was the mercy of God and the answering of her prayer.

As she grew in the Lord, she began to see it as

41

being very important to give my brother and me the Word of God and pray with us. We were younger, I can remember her having Bible studies with us at home. She would read the Bible and break it down on a level that we could understand. Some days she would round up several kids from the neighborhood and invite them over to our home for Bible study. She would teach them the precious Word of God and sometimes feed them a meal. It was important to her to teach us about God at home and not just take us to church and drop us off, leaving it to someone else to teach us. She didn't do everything right, but she loved and took good care of us.

I was no longer the little innocent boy she had raised in the church. I was a full time rebel at that time in my life. I was drinking alcohol, smoking weed, having sex with different girls, selling drugs, gang affiliated, lying, being disrespectful to my mother and other adults to the highest degree, and more. I was running from God and so in love with the world. I was living in darkness and I stopped going to church. I remember seeing the church van coming down the street some days and I would run and hide because I didn't want them to see me and convince me to get in the van. I told my mother that I no longer wanted to go to her church and that I wanted to go to the church down the street from our house where these pretty girls and some of my friends went. One day in my rebellion towards her, she got upset and chased me down the street. Thankfully, she didn't catch me because there's no telling what she would've done to me if she had caught me. Her Pastor prophesied to her one day and told her that she didn't have to worry about me anymore because God had me (in His hands).

I got upset with my mother one day and told her that King's family treated me better than she did and that broke her heart. Now I see how false that statement was because no one on this planet loved me more or sacrificed as much for me than my mother. At that time, I couldn't see that. Being in and of the world, my vision was blurred from seeing what was really true. I stayed away from home a lot and spent most of my days around King's house or in the streets somewhere. I would come home from time to time to get some food, sleep, take a bath, and change my clothes. Some days while being in the streets I wore the same clothes for a couple of days. I loved being around King's house because there were really no rules there. We sold drugs, smoked weed, used foul language, and stayed out as late as we wanted without anyone telling us that we couldn't. There were no real consequences for our actions. It felt like love, but I was actually running away from real love and that was the love that my mother gave me which came with truth and discipline.

My mother had gotten a rental car for transportation because we didn't have any at that time. She did this regularly because the rental company allowed her to rent cars at a very low rate once they got to know her better. Rich was still on drugs and one day he rented the rental car that my mother had out to someone in the neighborhood for drugs so that he could get high. My mother knew I was in the streets so she wanted me to go look for it one day. I really didn't know where to start looking around for it.

I can't remember how I ended up in a car with some of my friends from 'the block', but they had gotten a *"rental rock" (a car that is rented out for drugs)* and were riding in it most of the night having what we called fun. They were taking turns driving the car. I was riding around with them for a while before I was eventually dropped off at home that night. When the car was pulling off, my mother ran out of our house and yelled, "That's the car!" Wow! How high could I have been? Although she described the car to me, I forgot and had been riding around in the same car that I was supposed to be looking for. That same night, a guy from my neighborhood was murdered. The rental car that my mother had was included in the investigation because it was said that witnesses saw it being driven that night back and forth through the neighborhood around the time he was murdered. A detective came and picked the car up and took it to the crime lab to retrieve finger prints as evidence. Rich also became a suspect in the murder case and was arrested. Eventually, he was found not guilty and released.

I had gotten hired at a fast food restaurant around that time. I can't remember if I was fired or if I had quit the job but I didn't work there long. After working there for a few days, I went to work really high after smoking some *"dro/hydro" (high grade weed)* for the first time with a few friends and went to work and made a fool of myself. I believe that was my last day working there. I was messing up bad. I was steady following the crowd and being influenced by almost everything around me, especially money and what having money produced.

I remember riding around the neighborhood with Pédro one night. He had a Buick Road Master that had big rims on it and big speakers in the trunk. I wanted to be the one sitting behind the wheel cruising through the neighborhood in a car like that with everyone watching me. That's what I thought it meant to be successful. I saw *"dope boys" (guys who sold drugs)* in my neighborhood living what I thought to be the good life. They had the ladies loving them, the money, the latest clothing and shoes, the jewelry, the gold plated teeth, the clean old school cars with big rims and big speakers. They appeared to have all the power and was respected by many people. I wanted all those things and without it I felt like I wasn't successful. I saw that they were able to buy what they wanted when they wanted it. I wanted to be able to do the same, and in my young and wicked mind, there was only one way to make that possible... Money! Money would solve all my problems and make all my dreams come true. I understand now that I had made money my God, it had become my master. I worshiped it, served it, and was willing to do almost anything to obtain it **(Matthew 6:24)**. When it came to money, I wanted fast money not slow money. Since we had already committed a robbery a few weeks prior and had gotten away with it, it became an option in our minds on how to get more money fast.

> *"All black on, surrounded by individuals...*
> *That I did not really trust, I'm keeping it real with ya...*
> *dropped out of school, look at me, I'm a real fool...*
> *but ain't I fresh, ain't I 'G', ain't I cool?...*
> *I scored a lot, I thought I was winning, but ain't I lose?...*
> *I thought I was living life wide awake, but ain't I snooze?...*
> *acting wild, cursing loud, pants sagging, ain't I rude?...*
> *sin made me ugly, but them ladies called me cute...*
> *easy target, aim and shoot, I was slick, I was a flirt...*
> *dirty dog, did I mention Mama raised me in the church?...*
> *but going to church didn't make me 'saved'...*
> *but faith in the only One Who got out that grave...*
> *and clinging to the One Who lived, died, and raised...*
> *and trusting in that Name above every name..."*

◄ SECOND COUNT (ARMED ROBBERY) ►

We agreed to go and commit another robbery. We went back to the apartment complex where we committed the first robbery to look for the gun that Luke had thrown into the bushes, but we couldn't find it. If we were going to continue robbing, we needed another gun. Luke managed to steal a nine millimeter that belonged to Gold Mouth from out of the cabinet in the kitchen of his cousin's house. So once again, late one night, we were on the grounds of the apartment complex where we committed the first robbery. This time there was a fourth person with us, and his name was Slim. We waited for a while for someone to come down the hill in their vehicle and park so that we could rob them. Before anything happened, Slim backed out and said he had to go, so he left us. We should've all followed him, but our greed and lust for money was in full control of us so we stayed instead.

Finally we saw someone coming down the hill in their vehicle. As soon as the victim parked and got out, we approached the person. We then began yelling for the victim to give us the money. This time it was different, the victim started to scream very loud. I was not expecting that at all and fear of being caught gripped my heart. I was already afraid before it happened, but now it was real. We took a purse which included a little money, a cell phone, and other important things, such as credit cards and an ID and then ran back up the hill. Once we got back into our neighborhood, we went our separate ways. I made it home and went to bed not knowing that would be my last night sleeping in my own bed. Who was I kidding? I wasn't a robber, I wasn't a gangster, I was only a follower who following the crowd. Where was the crowd headed? Now I understand that I was following the crowd straight to hell. I had entered the wide gate and was traveling on the broad way full speed ahead.

Matthew 7:13-14 (NKJV) **"Enter by the narrow gate; for wide is the gate and broad is the way that leads to destruction, and there are many who go in by it. Because narrow is the gate and difficult is the way which leads to life, and there are few who find it."**

> *"I was shaped in iniquity...*
> *and in sin did my mother conceive me...*
> *it wasn't easy growing up in the hood, believe me...*
> *swimming with sharks that will eat you like a three-piece...*
> *so in fear I hit the block with the OG's...*

conforming to this world, Lord show me...
a way cause I don't want to live like this...
crack and marijuana balled up in my right fist...
it's not only about the money, I just want to be down...
I don't want to be lame, I don't want to be clowned...
what do I do to stop, I'm going deeper...
I feel so low so I get high on reefer..."

3

On the Run

The morning of May 23rd, 2002...

AS I WOKE UP each morning, my custom was to get high. I loved marijuana with all my heart and had to have it daily. My first experience with weed I believe was one night with my cousin Pooh and his friend. They were smoking and I joined in on the rotation. At that time, I was about fifteen and after that my life wasn't the same. I was addicted. Smoking weed became a "must do" in my life. I persistently pursued after it. Whether I was buying it myself, *"chipping"* on it *(going half with somebody)*, or just smoking what someone else had bought, I needed it. I couldn't live without it as far as I was concerned. I smoked almost daily and sometimes more than once a day. All my close friends were the same way. Even though we didn't acknowledge it back then, we were all addicted and our great need to have it and money drove us to do almost anything to get it.

The first time my mother saw me high was in the kitchen in our home on Empire Ave. I guess she either noticed the redness of my eyes or that my eyes were low, but she questioned me concerning them. I know she had hope and believed in God for my change. However, I believe she was very disappointed in the young man I was becoming. I was not a good example for my little brother. In the times that he needed a role model, I was in the streets all day and most nights chasing after the wind and wasting my life doing vain things. I was obeying the influences of the devil.

◄ THIRD AND FOURTH COUNTS (ARMED ROBBERY AND KIDNAPPING) ►

As I walked from my house to King's house that day, I saw my cousin Pooh in the midst of a crowd of people. He was about to fight a guy for touching his girlfriend inappropriately.

After the fight, King, Luke, and I gathered together and discussed committing another robbery although we had just committed one the night before. Who would be the one to stand up and say, "No, we don't need to keep doing this!" We called ourselves *"G's"* *(Gangsters)* and we had to prove that to one another. At least, I felt that way. We all agreed to do it again, but this time it would be different. This time it would be in broad daylight.

As we began to walk up Mutual Ave., Pooh asked me where we were going and I just told him that we would be back. Broad daylight? What were we thinking? I'm not sure, but I know what we were not thinking about and that was getting arrested. We didn't calculate it into our plans. We thought we were invincible. We thought we were too smart for the police. We thought we knew it all, but we were about to find out how much we didn't know. We were about to find out the seriousness of the consequences for our actions.

Our plan was similar to the other two robberies. We would wait until someone stopped, parked, and got out of their vehicle and then we would rob them and escape as before. We decided to go to a different location this time. As we walked, we passed by a house that was close to the end of the street we were on. We looked back and saw a person driving a car in our direction before turning into the driveway of the house we had just passed. The vehicle was parked behind the house. This person became our next target. I won't lie to you, I really didn't want to do this again. This time, I remember being scared. Honestly, I don't believe I wanted to do any of the robberies we had done.

We turned around and began to walk down the driveway and around the back of the house. I was surprised the person had walked into the house and left the back door wide open. I assume that the victim was either taking groceries or something else into the house and would probably come back to the car or close the door.

Since I hadn't held the gun in the last two robberies, I was supposed to be the gun holder this time. I got the gun and stood at the back door trying to build up some adrenaline to go into the house and get it over with. I was so afraid to do it, but felt I had to go through with it. I was too far in to back out and I didn't want to disappoint my friends, being the "people pleaser" that I was. I stood at the door for a long while, but I couldn't do it. I hesitated for so long that Luke took the gun from me and rushed into the house with King following him.

After a few seconds or so, I entered the house and both of them were already robbing the victim. No one saw me enter the house. I immediately went into another room and began to search for things such as jewelry, money, etc. In the midst of looking through the victim's dresser drawers, I heard the door that we entered in shut. It was quiet and my friends were gone.

I couldn't believe that I had been left alone in the house with the victim who didn't even know I was in the house. I walked out of the room and ran straight into the victim. The victim looked me straight in my eyes that were full of fear and probably heard my heart beating like a drum. We stood there for a moment in silence before I was asked, "Do you want to leave?" I don't remember saying a word but only nodding my head up and down signifying that I was saying, "Yes!" The victim opened the door for me and I ran like a cheetah trying to catch up with my friends.

Since King and Luke were unaware that I was in the house, they probably thought that I had *"chickened out" (not gone through with it)*. They had no idea that I was still in the house when they left.

◄ END OF THE ROAD ►

I ran for quite some distance. I was so tired and afraid of being caught by the police. It was still broad daylight and we were in the open and a good distance from home. Finally, I caught up with them. Luke hid the gun near his dad's house around the corner from where we were. We finally made it back our neighborhood and went to hang out at a friend's house. When we made it back to our neighborhood, I felt safe. We had done it again and gotten away with it. We were on a roller coaster with no brakes headed straight to destruction.

There we were on the front porch talking with our friend as if we hadn't just robbed someone. While sitting there, we noticed a police officer coming down the hill on Forest Ave. on a motorcycle and stopping at the four-way stop. The officer turned left onto Walnut St. toward *"Frank's Store"* then made a U-turn in the middle of the street and stopped at the four-way stop once again. When I saw him do this, I knew something was going on and fear gripped me. While the officer was at the four-way stop, he began to talk into the walkie-talkie radio that was on his shoulder. I also noticed that he had looked at us a few times while doing so. He then went straight forward through the four-way stop on Walnut St. and then he begin to do another U-turn in the middle of the street and head back to the four-way stop in our direction. By this time, I am fully aware of what was taking place and I jumped off the porch and began to run with all my might toward King's house. It was about five to ten minutes, running time, from where we were. King and Luke ran a different way, but we all ended upstairs at King's house.

Immediately, we began to change clothes as if that would help. I believe I had on all black, but I changed into some brown Dickies pants and a white Jamaican t-shirt. We looked out the window and saw a police officer outside asking the next door neighbor questions. We then began to hide in the room that we were in. The police was in hot pursuit of us. We were in trouble and had nowhere to run. They had us boxed in. It didn't take long for the street in front of the house to fill up with police officers, their vehicles, and people from the neighborhood. All of this for three young boys? I can imagine everyone from the neighborhood was wondering what was going on. The police came prepared. They were "locked and loaded". They believed that we were armed and dangerous and wasn't going to take any chances. We weren't armed and dangerous, we were full of fear and hiding.

The police soon came to King's house and entered in. This was a very heart gripping moment for me as a sixteen year old. As we walked down the stairs with our hands raised in surrender, they pointed their big guns in our direction with their fingers on the trigger. I know they were ready to squeeze the trigger if forced to do so. They slammed Luke down and an officer put his knee into his chest. He put a gun in his face and said, "This is what happens when you rob somebody!" Within minutes, we were all handcuffed and put into the back of separate police vehicles. It seemed as if the entire neighborhood came out to witness us being arrested. All eyes were on us, but we had no idea the severity of the consequences for what we had done.

◄ THE DETECTIVE BUREAU ►

A few weeks before all of this had taken place, I

was sitting in the *Macon Workforce Development* office in a class preparing to get a very promising job (more than just a summer job). Now, I'm sitting in the back of a police car heading to a place I had never been before and no one, not even my mother, could save me.

It wasn't long before the police car pulled up to *The Detective Bureau* downtown. We were taken into the building and the process began. My mother was at work when she received the call from a detective asking her if she had a son named Michael. She replied, "Yes!" She was shocked that she was receiving a call from them. The detective told her that I was in their custody and that she needed to come down to *The Detective Bureau* immediately. So she told her employer that she had to leave and she came downtown where we were.

At first, we all acted as if we knew nothing concerning the charges that were against us. The detectives began to ask us questions and get our statements concerning the charges we were facing. At that time, I didn't know that the officers weren't supposed to question us or get statements because we were under aged juveniles, minors. They were supposed to have waited until our parents arrived before they started interrogating us. Honestly, I believe they knew that very well, but at that point it didn't matter because they had the right guys for the robberies.

When my mother found out that I had been robbing people and had also been charged with kidnapping a person, she was shocked. It was unbelievable for her to hear those things about the son she raised in the church and taught the Word of God to.

We found out that the detectives linked the other two robberies to us as well. After my mother was there for a little while, they began to ask me more questions in front of her. They quickly let my mother know that I would not be going home with her, but that I would be staying there with them. She was very upset. King's mother was the only one who hadn't arrived. We were stuck for the long haul. That very same night we were taken to the *Macon Regional YDC (Youth Development Center)* and booked. The *Department of Juvenile Justice* would be our home for a while until we went to court.

We really didn't know the extremity of what we had been charged with nor the years that each charge carried. We thought that we would get off easy because we were only teenagers. We thought we were not old enough to go to prison. What was the worse they could do to us? After realizing the seriousness of our charges, we came together in the RYDC and made up a false story that we would tell the court. The story went something like this, *"While we were on the playground hanging out one day, a drug dealer pulled up in a green car, and pulled out a gun on us and forced us to sell drugs for him. We then did as we were commanded, but it didn't turn out well. So, we started robbing to get the money back for him because we feared for our lives..."* This lie didn't last long.

1 Timothy 6:9-10 (NKJV) ***"But those who desire to be rich fall into temptation and a snare, and into many foolish and harmful lusts which drown men in destruction and*** *perdition. For the love of money is a root of all kinds of evil, for which some have strayed from the faith in their greediness, and pierced themselves through with many sorrows."*

PART 2:

THE COCOON

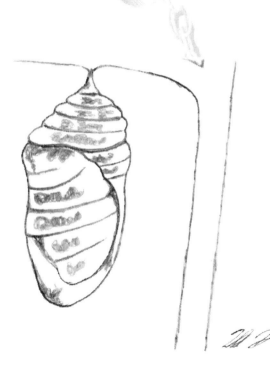

4

Plea Bargain

Summer, 2002... Locked up in the Macon RYDC waiting to go to court...

FOR THE LAST THREE MONTHS or so, the *Macon RYDC* was my dwelling place. I really missed being at home with my mother and brother. Upon my arrival, I didn't know what to expect. This was my first time ever being locked up. After being there for a while and getting the hang of things, I began to get a little understanding how the operation went. Honestly, we did have some good days in the RYDC, however, there were bad days also. I didn't forget that I was in jail and away from my family, neither did I forget that I had some heavyweight criminal charges against me and that I would have to go to court to face the judge soon.

There were a lot of boys and girls in there that I knew from the streets, but mainly from school. At that time, the RYDC housed boys and girls in the same building, but the boys were separated from the girls by hallways. We only saw the girls in the cafeteria or at other special events such as church service and school. Although we were incarcerated, we still had to go to school when we weren't on *"lock-down" (locked in our rooms for at least twenty-three hours a day)* for misbehaving.

We spent most of our time getting into trouble and rapping. King was the best when it came to rapping. He loved to rap. He had been rapping since around the age of nine. He was a strong influence in my life when I started to write rhymes and freestyle to music. We were very passionate about it. Before we got arrested, we were trying to record a CD together, but we ended up recording only one song. As time went by, we continued to get better with rhyming and we wrote a lot of verses and songs. We would make beats on the table or anything we could beat on with our hands and rap to the beat. We rapped about the things we loved, which was girls (sex), smoking weed, selling drugs, money, guns, gang affiliation, murder, etc. We glorified that lifestyle to the utmost degree and the other juvenile inmates loved the songs we would make. At times, we wrote positive songs mentioning God and church, although we were not living the way God wanted us to live. One day King wrote a song and some of the lyrics still stick with me even until this day. The lyrics on the chorus on the song were,

> *"I have been through the struggles...*
> *I have been through the pain...*
> *I have been through it all...*
> *But **JESUS** will pick you up when you fall..."*

◄ NOT GUILTY ►

One day I got into an altercation with an officer.

We tussled and I ended up with a busted lip. We were always insubordinate to the officers there, *"bucking"* on them *(disobeying and disrespecting them)*. After we had been indicted on the charges that were against us, we had to go to a few court hearings. We didn't believe that we would receive much time because we were only teenagers, but we had committed crimes worthy of us being charged as adults. That changed everything. We were charged with three counts of armed robbery and one count of kidnapping. We had done enough to receive at the very least about sixty years in prison.

> *We didn't realize that children could be prosecuted in superior court (as adults) even as young as the age of thirteen if they commit any of the "Georgia's Seven Deadly Sins" crimes, which are, murder, rape, armed robbery (with a firearm), aggravated child molestation, aggravated sodomy, aggravated sexual battery, and voluntary manslaughter. The law was passed in 1995. For a first felony offense, the law mandates at least ten years to be served without parole.*

At that time, my mother couldn't afford a lawyer for me so the court appointed me a lawyer. I received my first plea bargain from the court around that time and they offered to give me twenty years; fourteen to serve in prison and six to serve on probation when I was released from prison. My mother said they also offered to give me fifteen years altogether after that plea, but I don't remember. When I found this out, I remember breaking down and crying. I was only sixteen years old and they wanted to keep me in there until I was thirty.

When I was much younger and innocent, I never imagined myself going to prison in my future. It's amazing how life can turn out when we follow the wrong paths and run from God and His will for our lives. When I was out there *"wilding out" (living reckless)*, I didn't know that the time could be so weighty if I got caught. I don't believe we ever thought about getting caught and if we ever did we didn't believe that we would receive a lot of time because we were only juveniles. We were no longer just juveniles, we were juveniles charged as adults and we would be prosecuted and sentenced in the *Superior Court of Bibb County*.

One of *"Georgia's Seven Deadly Sins"* crimes is armed robbery with a gun and we had three counts. On September 4th, 2002, I went to court for an arraignment and pled not guilty to the charges that were against me. I knew I was guilty, but I lied because I did not want to receive all that time in prison. I refused to take responsibility for my actions.

I was unaware that my mother and her church family were praying for me. I'm grateful to have had someone in my corner supporting me. I don't even remember what my prayers sounded like back then. I'm sure I was begging and pleading with God to let me out. Although I was locked up, I was still in love with the world and God had no real place in my heart. I desired that He set me free from jail, but He desired to set me free from sin.

1 John 2:15-17 (NKJV) "Do not love the world or the things in the world. If anyone loves the world, the love of the Father is not in him. For all that is in the world— the lust of the flesh, the lust of the eyes, and the pride of life—is not of the Father but is of the world. And the world is passing away, and the lust of it; but he who does the will of God abides forever."

◄ THE ONLY FIGHT I GOT INTO ►

One day I got into a fight with a guy from Fort Valley, GA. It was a short fight because the officers broke us up quickly. Most of the fights that happened were initiated from foolishness. Sometimes a fight would start simply because you were not from the same city. The *Macon RYDC* held children from all over the Middle GA area and not just the city of Macon.

Macon, GA is known for its gang activity among so many other things. I knew of at least four major gangs/organizations at that time. They were the *"Crips"* (who wore blue), the *"Bloods"* (who wore red), the *"Gangster Disciples"*, also known as the *"Folks"* (who mostly wore black and sometimes dark blue), and the *"Mafia"* (who wore black). The RYDC held groups of young boys that represented every one of these gangs, so fighting among rival gang members was normal among us. Most of the fights or animosity were gang or either neighborhood affiliation related.

One day I was in the hallway leaning up against the wall when a different guy from Fort Valley walked up and punched me in the face. I almost fell to the floor. Immediately, the officers apprehended us. I was so mad and wanted revenge. I was cursing and trying to get loose so that I could retaliate, but they would not let me get to him. They ended up locking me down in my room for two days. I entered the room and began to kick on the door constantly making noise, but that didn't help. I wanted to hurt that guy so bad. "Why did I get locked down? He walked up and hit me!" I guess he was retaliating against me from when I fought his fellow Fort Valley friend. By the time I was released from lock-down, my adrenaline rush that I had to avenge myself was gone. Some of the inmates from Macon wanted to fight him, but I told them to let it go.

◄ GUILTY ►

Fall, 2002... Transferred to Eastman YDC...

King and I were transferred from the *Macon RYDC* to the *Eastman YDC* in Eastman, GA, leaving Luke behind. *Eastman YDC* was a male's only facility. We were placed in the Superior Court dorm where they held all the young boys from seventeen and younger who were charged with adult charges and waiting to go to court to be sentenced or released. One day almost everybody in the dorm was going to prison sooner or later unless they were acquitted of the charges against them. We met young men from all over Georgia in that dorm.

While I was there, my mother and some other family members visited me, and it meant a lot. When I was in Macon, I received quite a few visitations, but that changed now that I was in another city away from home. I stayed in Eastman for about a month before I was transferred back to Macon, GA, again to be sentenced on October 7th, 2002. I had a plea bargain hearing the day of my sentencing, and they offered to reduce all my charges (three counts of armed robbery and one count of kidnapping) down to only one count of robbery by force (without a weapon) altogether, but I would still be charged as an adult. My court appointed lawyer, who was a very good lawyer, negotiated with the Assistant District Attorney (The DA) concerning this plea bargain. When the DA found out that I wasn't the one holding the gun in either of the robberies, he agreed to offer me this lesser charge and this time I pled guilty. My co-defendants (King and Luke) made statements that corroborate to the fact that I didn't have the gun during any of the robberies. If I hadn't taken that plea bargain and instead attempted to take my case to trial, I probably would've never seen the outside of jail again. The judge would've found me guilty and "threw the book at me". They had too much evidence against us.

5

State of GA v. Michael Berrian Jr.

THE DREADFUL DAY had finally arrived and it was time for me to face the judge. All three of us were sentenced on the same day in separate courtrooms October 7th, 2002. At the ages of fourteen, fifteen, and sixteen, we were all prosecuted as adults.

When I entered the courtroom with my lawyer, I saw my mother and my uncle, Mo, waiting on us. They stood with me and my lawyer as we stood before the judge. I was so afraid! I knew I would not be going home that day and needed mercy from this judge who now had my life in his hands.

This is the official transcript from the day I was sentenced. I retrieved a copy of it from the clerk's office at the *Bibb County Courthouse* in Macon, GA. I removed the real names of the court officials, the victims, and my co-defendants. I also corrected the typos and grammatical errors that were in it.

State of GA v. Michael Berrian Jr.

Mr. Judge: Mr. District Attorney, whenever you're ready.

Mr. District Attorney: Yes, Your Honor.

This is indictment no. WXYZ67890. Count one charges Michael, Luke, and King with the offense of armed robbery, that the said accused on the 26th day of April, 2002, state and county aforesaid, did then and there with the intent to commit theft taken U.S. currency and a wallet, property of the victim from the person and immediate presence of the victim by use of a handgun which is an offensive weapon, contrary to the laws of said state, the good order, peace and dignity thereof.

Your Honor, counts two and three also charge Michael with armed robbery and count four charges Michael with kidnapping. The state has just submitted to Your Honor an order that nolle prosses those three counts due to the defendant's plea today to count one and count one will be a plea to robbery by force and I will get into, obviously, the facts behind that and why we're willing to do that today.

Are you the Michael Berrian named in this indictment?

Me: Sir?

Mr. District Attorney: Are you Michael Berrian?

Me: Yes, sir.

Mr. District Attorney: Speak up just a little bit louder.

Me: Yes, sir.

Mr. District Attorney: How old are you, Mr. Berrian?

Me: Sixteen.

Mr. District Attorney: Mr. Berrian, what's the last grade of school you completed?

Me: Eighth.

Mr. District Attorney: Do you read, write and understand the English language?

Me: Yes, sir.

Mr. District Attorney: Before coming to court today have you had any drugs, alcohol or any medications that would prevent you from understanding what's going on?

Me: No, sir.

Mr. District Attorney: I'll just ask you, do you understand what you're charged with?

Me: Yes, sir.

Mr. District Attorney: You understand I've been speaking with your attorney about you entering a plea today to one count of robbery by force?

Me: Yes, sir.

Mr. District Attorney: Do you understand what crimes and all that are surrounding that? Do you understand that?

Me: Yes, sir.

Mr. District Attorney: Do you understand if you plead guilty the court will impose some punishment on you today?

Me: Yes, sir.

Mr. District Attorney: If you plead not guilty, you have a right to a trial by jury. At this trial the burden would be placed on the state to prove your guilt beyond reasonable doubt. To do that the state would put up witnesses and evidence. You'd also have a right to subpoena witnesses and evidence in your own behalf. If we were to go to trial, you would have a right to ask your attorney through the subpoena power of the court to subpoena people to come to court and testify in your behalf. At this trial you'd have the right to be represented by a lawyer. If you could not afford a lawyer, one would be appointed to you free of charge.

You'd also have a right to a trial by jury. You could have a trial in front of a judge if you wanted to. You'd also have a right to testify at this trial. If you chose not to testify, however, that would not be held against you in any way. Do you understand these rights?

Me: Yes, sir.

Mr. District Attorney: Do you understand if you plead guilty today you're giving up... Well, let me back up real quick also. At this trial, if we were to go to trial and you were convicted, you'd also have a right to be represented by a lawyer at that appeal and if you could not afford one, one would be appointed for you free of charge also at that time.

Do you understand all the rights I've gone over with you?

Me: Yes, sir.

Mr. District Attorney: Do you understand if you plead guilty today you're giving up all these rights?

Me: Yes, sir.

Mr. District Attorney: Understanding this, do you wish to plead guilty or not guilty to one count of robbery by force?

Me: Guilty.

Mr. District Attorney: Are you doing so freely and voluntarily?

Me: Yes, sir.

Mr. District Attorney: Has anyone promised you anything or threatened you in any way to get you to enter a plea?

Me: No, sir.

Mr. District Attorney: Have you had an opportunity to speak with your attorney, Mr. Lawyer?

Me: Yes, sir.

Mr. District Attorney: Mr. Lawyer, have you had an opportunity to speak to your client?

Mr. Lawyer: I have.

Mr. District Attorney: Do you believe this plea is proper?

Mr. Lawyer: It is.

Mr. District Attorney: And do you believe he

understands his rights?

Mr. Lawyer: He does.

Mr. District Attorney: Will Your Honor accept this plea?

Mr. Judge: Give me a factual basis for the plea.

Mr. District Attorney: Yes, Your Honor. I will just address the count he's pleading to today.

Your Honor, on the 26th day of April of this year, the victim was returning home to his apartment. When he drove his truck into his parking lot and parking space, he was then subsequently approached by three young black males, two of them having handguns, one of them not. They demanded money from him which he gave them and they fled on foot. Actually two of them were on bikes at that time. One fled on foot and they escaped that night.

Now, I will go into a little bit of the other two counts and why the state is willing to enter a plea today to robbery by force, Michael was also charged with two other counts of armed robbery and kidnapping. Initially, I told Mr. Lawyer that I would not go below an armed robbery charge because I was under the false impression that Michael had a handgun during the last armed robbery that occurred, so that was my fault and it was corrected once Mr. Lawyer told me.

Statements given by this defendant and the other two defendants, however, corroborates the fact that

Michael did not have a handgun during the robberies. Michael, who did subsequent to his arrest, was given "Miranda" warnings. Michael, I believe, is fifteen.

Mr. Lawyer: Sixteen.

Mr. District Attorney: Sixteen now?

Mr. Lawyer: Sixteen now, yes.

Mr. District Attorney: Okay, and so, of course, he's at a young age. These are very serious charges, however, but that was the reason behind or the willingness on my part to let him plea to robbery by force and that we probably could have handled this earlier had this not been for my error in the facts of the case. It was my oversight.

I made an offer to Mr. Lawyer that he receive ten years with an eight year cap on service time with two years of probation to follow.

Mr. Judge: Okay. Michael, have you understood all the rights that you have to a jury trial, as Mr. District Attorney has just gone over with you?

Me: Yes, sir.

Mr. Judge: Do you have any questions about those rights you want to ask your attorney, Mr. Lawyer?

Me: No, sir.

Mr. Judge: You understand then that entering your plea of guilty you're waiving your right to a jury trial on this indictment and you're asking me to go ahead and sentence you on this one count which is reduced to robbery by force?

Me: Yes, sir.

Mr. Judge: You heard the facts as they were related to me by Mr. District Attorney.

Mr. Lawyer: I want to introduce as Defendant's Exhibit One, and I've given a copy of this to the State. It's a letter I'd like to ask the Court to look at. This is a letter he got at the time these robberies were occurring. This was what else was going on in his life, and it was a great opportunity... ...Which, Your Honor, he was not able to avail himself of by his own choosing by committing these acts with the other two boys. But he lives, as you can see, on Third Ave. (in Pleasant Hill). He's in a rough part of town. He goes to Central High School or he did. He was attending and doing well, as you can see from this letter.

So he has a future if he can just make the right choices to hang with the right people and if those people decide to do crimes to say, "No."

He has a good mother who cares about him and this is his uncle and each of them would like to say a few words on his behalf. I will also say that without any solicitation from me, Michael wrote letters of apology to the three victims. I asked him not to send them until we determine what to do about his case, but he sent them to me, and now that he's pleading I'll forward these on to the three folks involved. But they're heartfelt apologies from him for having done these deeds with these other two boys.

This is his mother, Mrs. Lennie, and his uncle, Mr. Lavender. Mr. Lavender is a Chief Instructor in the Navy and he'd like to say a few words and then his mother.

Mr. Judge: Sure. I'll be glad to hear from Mr. Lavender.

My Uncle: Your Honor and the Court, I'm Michael's uncle and I've been around him the majority of his life until the times I was sent overseas to the Middle East, and over in Japan and stationed always in California.

It's kind of hard sometimes to get back and forth to Georgia to try to be an influence on him. Just like Michael, I came through a neighborhood where there were a high poverty level and hardly any guidance. You can pull out your Roll-a-Deck and see all kind of black boys just like Michael coming of out theses rough areas. I was a pretty good product of one of those same individuals. I had went to jail one time, but once I was given the opportunity to change my life around, I did. Sometimes it's up to you and the DA to give some of the youth an opportunity because there is still time for rehabilitation. I believe if Michael is given the chance, he would utilize it to make something out of himself. He would be a more productive citizen than being behind bars where he would probably come out being worse and probably right back in within a year of coming out of that institution.

There's not much that I can say that would help what's already happened because everything is in your hands. I do ask for leniency on Michael and I will be more involved in his life than I have been. I'll try to make sure that happens.

Mr. Judge: Thank you very much, Mr. Lavender. I appreciate your sharing that with me.

Mrs. Lennie...?

My Mother: Yes, sir. I just want to apologize for his part and my part in it. My son, he's been through a whole lot in His young life. Both of us have. This is my third marriage and back in 1991 I was a recovering drug addict, but I thank God that the Lord changed me. I have two boys, my other son's name is Brandon and he is thirteen years old. We've been saved and in the church ever since nine years ago, and about four months ago he stopped wanting to go to church. He got with the wrong crowd and he just started hanging out and doing what other kids were doing. I talked and talked to him, but I guess they were more fun to be with than just being in the church.

I just thank God that he's not dead. By him going to jail, maybe that saved his life and I just thank God that he's... I'm not trying to say that he's better than anybody else's child, but I am saying that I believe that he's sorry for what he did. I really do believe he's sorry for what he did.

Mr. Judge: Thank you, Mrs. Lennie.

Mr. Lawyer: I think Michael himself may have a few words to say.

Mr. Judge: Sure. Be glad to hear from you, Michael.

Me: I'm sorry for what I did and I hope that all the victims are okay and I ask would you please be lenient on me.

Mr. Lawyer: One other thing I did explain to Michael and his mother was what the *"First Offender Act"* is, if the Court were inclined to grant it. Because he does have some promise of a future and tells me that He would like to go into the computer technical field one day. I know that a felony conviction may have some negative effect on those hopes and plans, so we do ask that you consider the *"First Offender Act"*. And I've explained both the good and the bad side of it to Michael.

Mr. Judge: Okay. Michael, the *"First Offender Act"*, I know Mr. Lawyer has gone over this in detail with you, but let me put it on the record just so I will know and you will know what we're dealing with here.

If you're sentenced as a *"First Offender"*, you only get this opportunity one time in your life. If I were to grant this request, and I'm not saying right this minute that I will because I'm still pondering that, but if I do grant this request I would be withholding adjudication.

I mean I would not be adjudicating you guilty of this offense of robbery by force, and if you fulfill all the terms of the sentence with no violations, then there would've never been an adjudication of guilt and you could honestly say that you don't have a felony conviction in your past. So on job interviews and application to schools, you could honesty say you don't have a felony conviction. There will always be a record of your arrest, the indictment, your plea of guilty to this count of robbery by force and the record of the sentence that's imposed. But there would be no adjudication of guilt.

Now, if during the term of the sentence you were to violate the law, for example, violate the sentence, the terms of the sentence and particularly if you were to commit a new crime, then you would be brought back to court on this case as well as the new case and on this the judge who heard the case could go ahead and adjudicate you guilty. I started to say revoke your sentence, but go ahead and adjudicate you guilty on this case and could impose that maximum punishment and require you to serve it in the penitentiary with credit for the time you successfully served. That would, on this case for robbery by force be twenty years.

So, if you violate the terms of the sentence that's about to be imposed, you could be brought back into court, again, the maximum punishment could be twenty years in the penitentiary with credit for time served before the violation. Do you understand that?

Me: Yes, sir.

Mr. Judge: So there is a great benefit If you don't ever violate the law again and you comply with the terms that are about to be imposed on a ten year sentence. On the other hand, if you violate the law, violate the terms of the sentence, you run a risk of twenty years in the penitentiary.

Now, understanding both the good and the bad with this kind of sentence, do you still want to be sentenced as a *"First Offender"*?

Me: Yes, sir.

Mr. Judge: Okay. Well, that means I would be placing my trust in you and that's not something that I generally do in cases of this kind of magnitude because while you're entering a plea to robbery by force, you were party, it appears from the indictment and the other charges, of more serious offenses that are being nolle prosses in return for this plea.

Anything further you would like to say?

Me: No, sir.

Mr. Judge: Okay. You've got good family support. I mean you're blessed to have a mother and an uncle willing to come stand with you here. A lot of people who come before don't have that sort of support and don't ever take it for granted.

Anything further, Mr. Lawyer?

Mr. Lawyer: That's it, Your Honor.

Me: Okay. Anything further, Mr. District Attorney?

Mr. District Attorney: Nothing further.

Mr. Judge: Bear with me just a minute.

Is there any restitution sought by any of the victims?

Mr. District Attorney: No, sir.

Mr. Judge: Is this an appointed or retained case?

Mr. Lawyer: I'm appointed, Your Honor.

Mr. Judge: And the evidence is clear Michael is not the one who had the pistol in any of these offenses?

Mr. District Attorney: Yes, Your Honor.

Mr. Judge: All right. Michael, on count one of this indictment, now reduced to robbery by force, I will sentence you to ten years. I will require that you serve four of that in incarceration and I will give you credit for the time you have already served in custody. Do you have that date, Mr. District Attorney?

Mr. District Attorney: It's been since May 23rd of this year.

Mr. Judge: With credit for time served since May 23rd of this year. That will mean that you will have six years to follow on probation. There will be a $1,000 fine and 200 hours of community service work. You will be required to reimburse the indigent defense office for the cost of hiring your lawyer and I will sentence you as a *"First Offender"*. You will be required to pay the probation supervision fees and statutory surcharges.

I don't lecture defendants who stand before me, so I'm not going to begin by lecturing you. But I'm counting on you and I know your mother and your uncle are counting on you too. You've been sentenced as a *"First Offender"*. So don't let any of us down, okay?

Me: Yes, sir.

Mr. Judge: Good luck to you.

Me: Thank you.

Mr. Lawyer: Thank you, Your Honor.

6

The Intermission

Romans 9:14-18 (NKJV) "What shall we say then? Is there unrighteousness with God? Certainly not! For He says to Moses (in Exodus 33:19), 'I will have mercy on whomever I will have mercy, and I will have compassion on whomever I will have compassion.' So then it is not of him who wills, nor of him who runs, but of God who shows mercy. For the Scripture says to the Pharaoh (in Exodus 9:16), 'For this very purpose I have raised you up, that I may show My power in you, and that My name may be declared in all the earth.' Therefore He has mercy on whom He wills, and whom He wills He hardens."

THE ONLY WISE GOD, in His sovereignty, chose to have mercy on me in that court room. I give Him all the credit, honor, glory, and praise for this! Even with my charges being reduced down to one count of robbery by force, I still could've received ten or more years to serve the full term in prison not including the time on probation that could possibly follow. King and Luke received their sentences the same day as I did. They both was sentenced fifteen years to serve; ten years incarcerated and five years on probation after their release from prison. They had also received a plea bargain for one count of armed robbery altogether (reduced from the three counts of armed robbery and one count of kidnapping we were charged with). God had mercy on them as well. So it was official, I wasn't going home until I was twenty years old and we would all be going to prison one day soon. This thought stayed with me while I continued to be housed in the *Macon RYDC*. I kept a calendar around that time and the time went by slooooow. I used to 'X' out days as they would go by.

A short while after being sentenced I was *"shipped off"* (transferred) to the *Savannah Regional YDC* in Savannah, GA. This RYDC was full of young boys and girls from Savannah and the surrounding areas. I was the only one there from Macon and there was also one guy from Columbus, GA. From being at the *Eastman YDC*, I was already familiar with some of the ways of those who were from Savannah and for the most part I stayed to myself. I didn't get into any fights, but if I had been from Atlanta, GA, it would've probably been a different story. I still don't understand why in the YDC or prison system that there is so much animosity between Atlanta and Savannah.

Savannah was over two hours away from home so I didn't get any visitations while I was there. I was there about a month and then I was shipped off to Milledgeville, GA, which was closer to home.

In late 2002, I arrived at the *Bill E. Ireland YDC* in Milledgeville, GA. This YDC was also a male's only facility and each dorm had its own color t-shirt that the juvenile inmates wore. I was placed in the "Cottage 12" dorm and we wore purple shirts. When I got on the campus I found out that there were a lot of inmates there from Macon, GA. Some of them I knew and some I didn't know. Nevertheless, it was encouraging to feel like I had somebody on my side. Being around people from your hometown was a bonus. In my dorm alone, there were several boys from my hometown and even one from my neighborhood, *Pleasant Hill.*

On my first night, there I was asked by an inmate, that we called ATL, if I smoked (cigarettes)? I told him that I didn't and that was pretty much the end of that. They would often sneak and smoke cigarettes and weed in the bathroom area. They would get it in from the officers, family, or friends through visitation or other ways (illegally). After a while of being there, I became friends with a lot of people in my dorm including ATL. One day we were talking and ATL asked me if I had remembered him asking me a few weeks before if I smoked and I told him that I remembered. He then told me that if I would've came into the bathroom to smoke that night that he and a few other inmates would've *"jumped"* me *(a fight where there is one against many)*, it was already planned out. As crazy as it seems, boys getting "jumped" on for no reason other than being "the new guy" happened a lot.

There were two big guys from Macon in my dorm that almost everybody respected, so being from Macon was a great advantage at that time for me. Both of them said they were members of the "Bloods" gang and I was friends with them both.

Major cities (and their surrounding areas) stuck together and most times when you had a problem with someone from a certain city, then you had a problem with everyone from that city. The major cities were Atlanta, Macon, Savannah, Valdosta, Albany, Columbus, and Augusta, GA. While I was housed in Milledgeville, a few riots took place mostly between inmates from Atlanta and Savannah. Macon was involved in a riot one day, I believe it was against Atlanta. I decided that I wasn't going to participate in it because it had nothing to do with me. Most people will act all tough and get something started then want you to be a part of the aftermath. Although, I had planned that I wasn't going to be a part of it, I was still preparing to defend myself against anyone that would come in my direction to harm me simply because I was from Macon. My knowledge of what happens in riots of this magnitude had me hesitant because I knew that someone could really get hurt or even killed in the midst of it and I didn't want it to be me. I didn't want to get stabbed, hit in the head with a brick, or "jumped" by multiple inmates. Riots could start anywhere at any time. Although I was still a follower, I wasn't about to follow anyone into that riot. I believe it was in this YDC that I finished reading the entire Bible cover to cover, but I still didn't know God.

> *"The judge sentenced me 'ten do four'...*
> *It was heavy on my back like carrying two folks...*
> *sixteen with an adult charge on my way to prison...*
> *those of you who have ears to hear, I hope you're listening..."*

Winter, 2003...

My seventeenth birthday was approaching and I knew that I would be leaving the YDC and going to prison soon. By that time, King and Luke had already been shipped off to prison at the ages of fifteen and sixteen. Regardless of me knowing that I would be going to prison one day, there was still hope in my heart that I would be allowed to finish my sentence in the YDC. The most time you could do in the YDC was five years, so with me only having a little over three years left to serve I thought I might be able to stay. There was one thing different about my case than most of the boys at the YDC and that was I was charged as an adult and not a juvenile.

January 31st came and went and I was still sitting in the YDC. I thought I had gotten away, but one cold morning a few days after my birthday I was called to pack up my things because I was being moved. I was taken to the ship off area where I saw a big red and white bus waiting for me. The *"GDC" (Georgia Department of Corrections)* officers had come to pick me up and transport me to prison. They shackled me down in chains connected to handcuffs that were put around my wrists, waist, and ankles and then they told me that I had graduated to the big boy's camp. My seat was in the front of the bus and as far as I know, I was the only youth on the bus. There was no turning back at this point, I was now in the hands of a God.

About an hour or so later we pulled up at

Georgia Diagnostic Prison located in Jackson, GA. We stayed there for more than an hour and then I was put on another bus heading to *Lee Arrendale State Prison*, better known as *"Alto"*. I didn't know what to expect, but there was no turning back. I was property of the state now and on my way to the concrete jungle.

7

1126382

Mug shot: 17 years old, 2003.
Day one, ("Alto") Lee Arrendale State Prison, Alto GA.

WE RODE FOR ABOUT TWO HOURS on the bus before we arrived at "Alto" (*Lee Arrendale State Prison*). The prison is located in the north GA area in the city of Alto. This is where I would spend the next two years of my life. "Alto" housed men of all ages including young boys that were seventeen years of age and younger who had committed one or more counts of the *"Georgia's Seven Deadly Sins"* crimes.

After we got off of the bus and entered into the prison, the guards had us strip and shower in the open for all to see. Then, we were assigned our prison clothes which consisted of white pants and shirts with blue stripes, white boxer shorts, t-shirts, socks, and black boots. We were also given a blanket, sheets, and a pillow for the bed we would be assigned to. All of the hair on our heads was cut off, it was as bald as they could cut it. We were all given a *Georgia Department of Corrections* number that we would be identified by and mine was 1126382.

"Alto" was a huge prison and had three units (A, B, and C units) on its premises. Each unit consisted of multiple buildings and some of the buildings consisted of more than one "dorm" *(dormitory)* on the inside of it.

The diagnostics dorm was inside A-unit and all inmates seventeen years old and older had to go through the dorm for about six weeks before going into general population. During those six weeks many tests were given to determine the area you were housed. In A-Unit there were three different buildings. One of the three buildings housed the diagnostic inmates (new inmates), the seventeen year old young men, and the juvenile boys (sixteen years of age and younger). These groups of inmates were separated by dorms. The second building in A-unit housed inmates who had been there for a while and had good behavior or either low security. The last building was called "the annex building".

After my diagnostics period was over, I was put in the seventeen year old dorm. All the rooms in the dorm I was assigned to were "two men cells" and were comprised of one bunk bed (two beds, top and bottom), two locker boxes, one toilet, one sink, one mirror, and one window. The doors to the rooms were power-locked and controlled by the officers in the control tower. Once the doors were locked, it could only be opened again from the control tower in the building.

King and Luke had already been in "Alto" for a few months before I arrived. They were in the same building where I was housed, but in a different dorm because they were under seventeen years of age. I was often able to see them in passing from time to time. At all times, the officers kept the juvenile inmates separated from the rest of the prisoners. Usually, the seventeen year old young men were housed in the seventeen year old dorm until around the time of their eighteenth birthday. However, I've seen seventeen year old inmates sent across the yard before their eighteenth birthday because of their behavior or inadequate space, I believe.

I had just turned seventeen a few days before I

arrived at the prison so I stayed in the seventeen year old dorm for several months. I knew one day I would be going across the yard, but I dreaded it because I didn't know what I would possibly encounter when I got there. I only heard about some things that went on across the yard and it was not good, especially for a new, young, and inexperienced prisoner such as myself.

I was comfortable being housed in the seventeen year old dorm and I became friends with a lot of the young men there. They were from all over GA, even my hometown.

When the officers were not walking around patrolling the dorm, inmates were fighting, smoking weed and cigarettes, and tattooing to name a few things. I was still in the seventeen year old dorm when I got my first prison tattoo. The tattoo was my mother's first name, *"Lennie"*, written in cursive with a heart as the dot of the 'i'. I got two more tattoos later on, one on each of my arms, *"MAC"* on my right arm and *"TOWN"* on my left arm (*"Mac-Town"* is a nickname for Macon, GA). Some of the inmates were very smart and creative. They could make a tattoo gun from the motor of a tape player. By the time King and Luke had served their ten year sentences, they collectively had gotten over 100 tattoos on their bodies from their necks to their waistlines.

There were a lot homosexual activities that took place all over the prison including the seventeen year old and juvenile dorms. Inmates would talk to other inmates as if they were girls. This resulted in a lot of fights and other violent activities. Although, some young men may have been playing, but some of the other young men took it more seriously.

A lot of the young guys in the dorm I was in were serving some heavyweight time. Most of them would be in prison for the next ten years, some ten to twenty years plus, and a few would probably never be going home because of a "life sentence". There were many that only had about ten years or less and I was one of them only having to serve about three more years myself. "Across the yard" I ran into inmates that had so much time to serve it was unbelievable. I knew of guys who had received three life sentences, four life sentences, two life sentences plus forty years, and 380 years for crimes they committed. I am not sure of how truthful these inmates were about their sentences, but I do know that they couldn't possibly serve that much time. It was evident that they would probably never see the free world again as free men unless a miracle from God took place in their lives. At that time, I was still young and wild. No genuine regard for man nor God, I was still trying to fit in with everyone else. I was still being a follower, I was still in the fast lane, heading towards destruction.

> *"Growing up, I really did believe that I was right with God...*
> *I didn't know the lifestyle that I lived was fighting God...*
> *professing to be a Christian, I was not, I was not...*
> *I was hot, I was on the block, I was selling rocks...*
> *smoking weed, getting high, drinking just to get by...*
> *having sex, giving myself away but not to God...*
> *I said I was saved but not once did I show it...*
> *I was living in the dark and I didn't even know it..."*

I began to go to the church services that were being held in the chapel of the prison, but I quickly stopped because the services wasn't like the services we had back at home. The chapel services were dull from my point of view. I was raised in a holiness church and was used to the upbeat music and energetic preaching that went on there. I guess I was what most people call religious or spiritual in ways, but I know now that I didn't have a real relationship with Christ when I was professing to be a Christian back then. At that time, I was God's enemy according to **James 4:4** because I was still very much a friend of the world.

I was raised in what I would call a "Christian-like" household due to my mother being saved in 1991; I was around five years old when she became a Christian. My younger brother and I was introduced to the Christian way, the Bible, prayer, and church through my mother's relationship with the Lord. I was just like a large portion of others in the world today, professing to be someone who I truly wasn't. I often said I was a Christian, but my words and actions did not connect together. They were totally different from one another. Therefore, it was easy for me to just say I was a Christian although I wasn't living like a Christian. Honestly, I didn't 'know' God at all, I only 'knew about' Him. I guess I thought that duties such as going to church, knowing Bible scriptures, and praying was knowing (having a relationship) Him outside of simply surrendering my life unto His Lordship and doing His will (**Luke 13:24-27**). I was wrong and I understand now that there's a big difference in the two.

I knew that **JESUS** existed. Although sinless, He died on a cross for the sins of the whole world. He was raised from the dead. He healed the sick. He had twelve disciples. His mother's name was Mary and she was a virgin when she had Him. He was betrayed by Judas Iscariot. He was God's only begotten Son, and the list goes on. All these things are good to know and are true, but knowing these things about Him doesn't mean that I knew Him personally. **JESUS** said, *"If you love me, keep my commands...and I will love you, and manifest myself to you"* (**John 14:15, 21**). It starts with knowing Him, which leads to loving Him, which leads to obeying Him. They are one in the same.

So, if I truly profess that I am a Christian (a follower of **JESUS** Christ) and lived a lifestyle that did not reflect that, does it still make me a Christian? Am I a Christian only because I say I am? Absolutely not. **JESUS** asked this question one day, *"Why do you call me 'Lord, Lord' and not do the things which I say?"* (**Luke 6:46**). I did not know God, but at that time I didn't know it. I believed I was a Christian because I was raised around Christian activities. I knew Bible Scriptures by heart and I knew how to pray. I learned and 'knew about' God, but I didn't 'know' God! I was living my life like everyone around me, in sin. I didn't understand the importance of my lips and actions being in sync. So many people profess to be Christians, but in their daily actions they deny Him.

1st John 1:5-7 (NKJV) "...God is light and in Him is not darkness at all. If we say that we have fellowship with Him, and walk in darkness, we lie and do not practice the truth. But if we walk in the light as He is in the light, we have fellowship with one another, and the blood of JESUS Christ cleanses us from all sin."

◄ ACROSS THE YARD ►

Education (school) was a big part of the prison as well. Either you went to school or to a "detail" (work) Monday through Friday. If you didn't go to where you were assigned to go, you were put in the "hole" *(lockdown; solitary confinement twenty-three hours a day with one hour of recreation time in a small one man fenced-in area)*. I went to school and worked on obtaining a GED.

After seeing the young men that I was in the dorm with being sent "across the yard" little by little almost weekly, the day finally came that it was my turn to go. I was sent to C-Unit. C-Unit was very different from A-Unit. This unit of the prison was an "open dorm" unit (no locked doors to the rooms). Every room was connected to another room that had three bunk beds on each side, three per room (six inmates on each side). The rooms were connected by a bathroom in the middle that consisted of toilets, a large sink, one open shower with no door to it and a big window. When using the restroom or shower, everybody that walked by could see you. There was no privacy unless you created some by hanging something up to cover the window or shower.

There were four dorms in C-Unit, 15, 16, 17, and 18, which held about ninety-six inmates a piece. I was housed in dorm 15. I met a lot of people in this dorm from my hometown and other areas of Georgia that I befriended. Some were laid back (good, positive guys) and kept to themselves, and most of them were trouble makers and stayed into something. One of the good guys was named Q, he became a good friend of mine while I was in that dorm. He was very talented in the area of spoken word/poetry and he could also rap. His lyrics were like no other I've heard even until this day. It was jaw dropping how he creatively put words together and although he was sentenced three life sentences, he didn't wear it on his sleeves. I never saw him walking around like he was "mad at the world" because of the time he had to serve. He introduced me to some other inmates that I would come to befriend as well. They were his "brothers" and into the Bible, church, and stuff like that. Brothers like Los, TJ, and Ro-Mill.

Two of my closest friends in the dorm were Pitts and Lackey. They were both serving a ten year sentence for armed robbery. Like many others, I knew both of them from the seventeen year old dorm in A-unit and was comfortable around them although they stayed into trouble. Pitts, Lackey, and I hung out all the time. Almost daily we would play cards, dominoes, write rhymes and rap. All of us could rap pretty well although the messages in our songs was wicked. Sometimes we would stay up all night hanging out, sipping "Bombay" (*coffee, Kool-Aid, soda and jolly ranchers mixed together*), smoking cigarettes, and telling stories about the lives we lived in the "free world" before we were arrested and what we will do once we were released from prison. We use to call those conversations "*getting out there*". These were my friends and we looked out for one another, but there was one thing they did that I didn't want any involvement in. Sometimes they broke into other inmate's locker boxes and stole their goods from them.

I was keeping the wrong company (affiliation). I didn't quite understand how much my life was in danger simply because of who I was hanging with. I remember hearing about a guy whose head had been busted open with a "lock in a sock" *(combination lock that was put in a sock and used as a weapon)* for stealing something from someone. When you are a known thief, you can expect people to come to you first when something is stolen, whether you did it or not.

Affiliation with the wrong person or people can get you into serious trouble, more prison time, hurt or even worse, killed.

1st Corinthians 15:33 (AMP) **"Do not be so deceived and misled! Evil companionships (communion, associations) corrupt and deprave good manners and morals and character."**

8

Wasting My Life

One day Lackey decided to break into Bo's locker box while everyone else was at "chow call" *(dinner)* and then he put all of the stolen goods into Pitts' locker box to hide it (Pitts was unaware of it as well as myself, as far as I can remember). That day there was a baseball game going on out on "yard" (the recreation area) and that's where Pitts was, he had gone there immediately after "chow call". Lackey ended up on the yard as well and that would be his alibi.

Bo was a "lifer" *(an inmate with a life sentence)* and was not the one to be stealing from. A guy named Port began to spread the word about the incident and it reached the ears of Bo that Lackey and Pitts had broken into his locker box and taken his goods.

From where I was standing, I saw a guy from my hometown pass Bo a "shank" *(a knife or a sharp weapon)* which looked to me like a screw driver, and then immediately he begin to hunt for Lackey and Pitts (although Pitts had nothing to do with). I began to think something on the lines of this thought, *"Everybody knows we are close friends... But they are known for stealing... Maybe everybody thinks I'm a thief*

---

too..." So to me, Bo looking for them meant that he was looking for me as well because of our affiliation. I knew he wasn't coming to sit down and talk with us about it over a cup of coffee, he was coming for blood and I was fearful of being stabbed to death. I didn't have a "shank" to defend myself with nor do I believe I could have fought him off of me.

Lackey and Pitts were still outside on the yard while Bo was searching for them on the inside of the dorm. As he walked down the hall looking into the rooms, I could see that he wasn't playing around at all. He was serious about making an example out of them both for stealing from him. I can imagine he felt disrespected to the highest level. In prison, if someone steals from you and you find out who did it, it was a must that you do something about it whether it was fighting them, stabbing them, busting their head with a "lock in a sock", or something worse. You could easily let it go and do nothing about it, but you would risk the chance of other inmates thinking that you were a "free pick" *(someone that they could do anything to with no consequences)*. This could result in many more inmates stealing from you, robbing you by force, or making effort to sexually assault you.

As I stood in the hallway, I saw Bo angrily walking down the hallway in my direction still searching for them, he was focused like a bull charging at a red flag. As he got closer to me, fear gripped my heart to the point of holding me captive and I stood still thinking that my life was about to possibly end. When he reached me, I backed up against the wall to brace myself for defense. My heart was beating hard and it felt as if my heart had dropped down into my boot. I was so afraid and didn't know what to do at that moment to defend myself from someone who was bigger than me, stronger than me, and carrying a weapon that could kill me.

To my surprise, he walked right past me as if he didn't even see me. By this time Lackey and Pitts had made it back into the building. When Bo saw them he instantly went after Pitts, swinging the "shank" at him and missing. Pitts got away by running back outside the building. After that, he swung it at Lackey and struck him in the chest slightly, but not hard enough for it to penetrate very deeply. Lackey's back was against a door to one of the rooms so he went through it defending himself the best way he could while Bo was persistently chasing after him trying to stab him. Lackey managed to run through the room he was nearby. Bo chased him through the room, the bathroom, and out the door on the other side of the room back into the hallway. Lackey then ran out the main door to the outside of the building where he ran into Pitts, who was on his way back in to help him (Pitts thought that Lackey had ran out the building right behind him). When Bo got near the door that leads to the outside, he was apprehended by one the correctional officers. He dropped the weapon on the floor and he was placed in handcuffs and taken to the "hole". Although Lackey's shirt was bloody from the small puncture wound, he escaped with his life. When the officers found out what really happened, they came and took Lackey and a few others and put them in the "hole", but they missed Pitts. When Pitts found out that Port was the one who told Bo that he and Lackey had broken into the locker box, he went looking for him. When he found him, he begin to mercilessly beat him with his fists. The officers took Pitts and Port to the "hole" as well after that.

God had mercy on me yet again and I believe he hid me from the wrath of Bo. I could've died that day right there in the hallway. Having the wrong affiliation almost got me killed.

◄ CD PLAYER BLUES ►

While I was still in the seventeen year old I had gotten into some trouble and was sent to the "hole". I was put into a room with an inmate named Tray until a room was available for me, I'm guessing that the "hole" was fully occupied. As I sat on the floor of this one man cell, I conversed with this stranger and hours later I was put into my own cell. A short while after that an "orderly" *(an inmate that works around the prison)* came to my cell and told me that Tray asked to borrow my radio. At that time, I didn't see anything wrong with lending my radio to him for a while. So, I handed it to him through the bars of my cell not knowing that I would never see it again. Tray had really gotten over on me. He had no intentions of returning my radio and being locked behind the barred cell I couldn't get to him to retrieve it. I didn't see Tray again until months later when he was transferred to C-Unit and I wanted to hurt him for taking my radio as if I was a "free pick". I thought about waiting until he went to sleep and getting a yellow mop bucket wringer and swinging at his head with all my might. That would've taught him a lesson, right? I decided to just let it go instead of continuing to hold a grudge against him and I risked the chance of other inmates thinking I was prey.

On another occasion while in C-Unit, someone went into my locker box one day and stole my CD player. I didn't expect that to happen to me. I had been in the dorm for a few months and had become comfortable with a lot of the inmates to the point that I stopped locking my locker box. I let my guards down. After it was stolen and the word began to spread about it, a lot of the inmates that I was associated with came to me saying that they would help me look for it and they would handle the inmate who had done it. I spoke up and told them not to worry about it. Some of them may have looked at me as someone who they could take advantage of, but I was thinking to myself, "One of you all may be the one that took it."

I stayed in C-Unit for several months, but because of the few write ups I received for bad behavior, I was sent to B-Unit, a more high security (high max) unit. I remember three buildings being in B-Unit, each with two dorms on the inside of each one. I was placed in dorm E-2. The rooms in this unit were two men cells which were comprised of one bunk bed, two locker boxes, one toilet, one sink, and one mirror. The doors to the rooms were controlled by the officers in the control tower just like in A-Unit. I ran into some of the young men that I was in the seventeen year old dorm with and more inmates from my hometown while in B-Unit. Around that time, I started feeling like I had the hang of things. I tried my best to stay out of the way of harm although it was almost impossible to do so in the environment I was in. I stayed away from gambling, borrowing stuff, and hanging with inmates that I didn't know. I mostly hung with inmates that were from Macon or the surrounding areas, however, there are quite a few inmates who were not from my hometown that I befriended because they seemed to be some decent guys. I spent most of my time listening to music, writing raps, and rapping in cyphers we would have from time to time. I really didn't like playing basketball either but I watched sometimes. I had stopped going to church completely around that time. I don't even believe I was reading the bible or praying at all anymore. If I was, it wasn't much. I was just doing time the best way I knew how, apart from a real relationship with God.

◄ YOUNG MAN MURDERED NEXT DOOR ►

Winter, 2004...

One early Sunday morning, a while after lock-down time which is 1 AM on the weekend, I looked out the window that was on the door to my room and saw a vehicle that resembled an ambulance with "GBI" *(Georgia Bureau of Investigation)* on the side of it parked outside in the front of my building. A while after that, I saw a stretcher with an inmate laying on it being wheeled out from E-1 (the dorm next door) towards the

"GBI" vehicle. It was someone that I knew from the seventeen year old dorm. I was puzzled and didn't know what was going on and I wanted to know. Something was definitely wrong, this had to be serious. Later that morning after it was time for us to come out of our rooms again, the news begin to spread around about what happened to the young man and I couldn't believe it. The young man was now dead, he was only eighteen years old. He didn't just die of a natural cause, he was senselessly murdered by three inmates who were attempting to rape him. In the midst of him being strangled and assaulted, his wind pipe was crushed and he died. After hearing the awful news, a thought dawned on me. I thought something like this, *"You can come to a place like this and never make it back home."* I began to see things differently after that. Prison was not a game and I needed to be more serious about life and making it back home.

According to public writings about this case that I've read online, it was planned out by the three inmates. They planned to enter his cell, choke him into unconsciousness, and have sex with him. They rigged the door so that they could easily slip out of his room afterward, but something went wrong with the rigging of the door and they ended up being locked in the room with him. An officer found them in the room and all three of them were eventually tried in a court of law for the murder of the young man and received a life sentence, with no possibility of parole. That doesn't suffice the pain and hurt caused to his family for the loss of his life though.

◄ HOMOSEXUALITY IN PRISON
(VOLUNTARILY AND INVOLUNTARILY) ►

*I am sharing my point of view about this topic according to what I have heard and saw while being incarcerated, other documents I've read about prison, and documentaries I have seen about prison. I never saw anyone being raped while I was in prison. I only heard stories and knew of inmates that were either the predator or the prey in such cases.

The young man I knew wasn't the only victim of such a heinous crime as this. A lot of homosexual activity and rapes by individuals and multiple inmates goes on in the prison system not only in GA, but all over America. *Dan Harris (of ABC News) wrote an article January 7th, 2006 called "Prison Rape widely ignored by Authorities". He stated that more than 200,000 men are raped behind bars each year, according to the group 'Stop Prisoner Rape'. While rape under any circumstance is a violation, human rights advocates say rape in prison is also torture.* "Alto" was known for new, young inmates being the prey of either older inmates or inmates that were young but had been in prison for a number of years already and had embraced that type of mentality and lifestyle of being a predator. I believe a lot of the rape victims don't tell the authorities that they are being preyed on or have already been assaulted because of fear of what their sexual assaulter may do to them. Some of them may tell the officers in authority, but sometimes there is nothing done about it. I believe some inmates who are considered prey may eventually just give in to the pressure of the predator over time out of fear, and would participate in it willingly. Although some prey are forced to have sex and could be raped without their consent. After an infirmary (hospital) visit, there's a possibility that the victim would be put back into general population over time and there is a greater possibility that it could happen again. Some inmates request "PC" *(protected custody)*, but making that decision doesn't guarantee their safety, as in the case of the young man that I spoke about who was murdered. He contacted his family and told them he was being sought after by inmates who wanted to have sex with him. His family contacted the prison and requested that he be kept safe through protected custody, but he was kept in general population anyway and eventually died there. Some inmates, after being raped or just giving in to homosexual activity willingly, could possibly be forced (to) or willingly continue living that lifestyle until their release from the prison. Even if they were to be transferred to another prison and someone that knew they were a "boy" *(someone's punk)* then they possibly would be approached in that manner all over again. Some inmates are not only raped but beaten or threatened first. It is very possible for inmates to get knives or other sharp objects that could be used as a fear tactic in order to rob someone for their "store goods" *(food bought from the prison store; commissary)* or rape someone. Some predators in prison will rape their victims and then threaten to harm or kill them if they ever told the officers about it.

There were some men who actually dressed up as

women the best they could with make-up, arched eye brows, glossy lips, and long nails. Some would purposely talk in a higher pitched tone as to sound like a woman. Some of them looked and carried themselves as regular men even though they were involved in that type of activity. Most of the time you never knew who was involved in homosexual activity unless the word had spread about them. There were also actual couples in there. I remember next door to me there was two inmates in a relationship, and one of them was named after a fruit.

Most inmates were under the impression that if you were a predator that it was ok. It was like the predators weren't really considered homosexuals, but if you were the prey you were a considered a punk, a "boy", or a woman.

In the eyes of God, who made man and woman, it is an abomination for a man to rape or have consensual sex with another man, and it's the same with women who rape or have consensual sex with other women. The laws around the world may change, but God's law is unchangeable.

It's really heart breaking to know that this goes on constantly in the prison system all over America and probably all around the world regardless of the "PREA" *(Prison Rape Elimination Act)* law. From my recent research, I found out that homosexual activity in the women's prisons are on a high level as well. A rapist and homosexual spirit was all over "Alto", but I thank God for keeping me from it. I want to be the first to say that it wasn't because I was a great fighter, nor because I had a big knife in case somebody tried to come after me, nor was it because I deserved God's protection. It was only the sovereign, loving, and merciful hand of the Lord God Almighty protecting me and keeping me from that lifestyle. I would not have survived my time in prison had not it been for God keeping me in His hands despite me constantly doing things my own way. I would've been beaten, I would've been raped. I would've been stabbed. I would've been killed. I would've never seen the outside of prison again had not it been for **JESUS** Christ watching over me to perform His Word in my life. Whether He was doing it for me or just answering the prayers of those that were faithfully praying for me, I am grateful and forever in debt to Him for the rest of my life. I can't answer the question why, but

Romans 1:24-31 (NKJV) "...God also gave them up to uncleanness, in the lusts of their hearts, to dishonor their bodies among themselves...God gave them up to vile passions...Even their women exchanged the natural use for what is against nature. Likewise also the men, leaving the natural use of the woman, burned in their lust for one another, men with men committing what is shameful...God gave them over to a debased mind, to do those things which are not fitting..."

◄ **DRUGS IN PRISON** ►

Whether it was through visitation or a correctional officer, it was easy to get weed into the prison. I never saw any other drugs besides weed in there, but I'm sure there were other drugs in there like cocaine because different inmates were addicted to different drugs on the streets before coming to prison and with money, almost anything is possible to get. Some officers will do almost anything for a little extra money, including risking the chance of losing their job and being arrested for bringing illegal contraband onto the campus. Some inmates risk being put into the "hole" or receiving a new charge that will require them to go to court and be sentenced for it, adding more punishment to their current sentence.

At that time in "Alto", a $5 bag of weed costed $50 from the seller. Can you imagine if an inmate managed to get in an ounce or pound of weed inside of the prison and began to distribute it? A lot of illegal drug dealing went on and a lot of money was made. It was easy to sell because almost everybody wanted it. Store goods was the equivalent of money in there. I never managed to get any weed in personally, but every now and then I was able to smoke weed due to other inmates that I knew who were getting it in through their source. I believe it was one day around Christmas when an inmate that I had befriended managed to get his hands on a real cigar. That was the first time I smoked a real blunt inside of prison, other than that it was always a small joint rolled up in cigarette paper.

Some of the inmates would bring fruit from the cafeteria and store it up in jugs for weeks until it fermented before drinking it. We called it "Buck", it was like moonshine. Also drinking coffee with Benadryl in it or "Bombay" were other ways inmates sought to get some kind of high or buzz.

9

Getting My Attention

◀ RAMEN NOODLES ▶

I was able to go to the store some weeks when my family sent me money. It was always a blessing to be able to go to the store call. We were only allowed to spend up to $60 a week at the store. Items on the store list included hygiene products, various kinds of food, snacks, drinks, tobacco products, stamps, envelopes, and more. Although there was a great variety of food that could be purchased from the store, Ramen noodles, honey buns, and sodas were at the top of my list. I was raised on Ramen noodles but while in prison I really fell in love with them, it became a delicacy to me. My favorite was the creamy chicken flavor Ramen noodles and I could eat them every day. My second favorite snack from the store was the honey buns. I would spread peanut butter across the top of them and eat them. They were so delicious.

Although I was very slim, I "worked out" (exercised) and ate Ramen noodles and honey buns with peanut and yeast sprinkled on it attempting to gain some weight. Some days I would trade my chicken dinner for a Ramen noodle or two. I had grown tired of eating the buzzard sized chicken leg quarters every week. One of my favorite meals from the kitchen menu was what we called "Shank" (hot sausage and gravy poured over biscuits), but even that wasn't more mouthwatering than a pack of Ramen noodles. There were so many ways to fix up the noodles. I ate Ramen noodles with pepperoni, hamburger, rice, pickle, black beans, potato chips (of all kinds), cheese crackers, beef and cheese stick, and much more. There were times when I couldn't go to the store due to me not receiving money most weeks from my family or because I was on restriction for receiving a "DR" (disciplinary report; write-up) for bad behavior. On those weeks I was only allowed to buy things such as stamps, envelopes, note pads, and pens. In those times, I would mostly buy stamps and mostly sell them for Ramen noodles.

Some days we would come together and make what we called a "pizza" (a large amount of Ramen noodles put into one big bag mixed with all kinds of ingredients). Many of us would come together and make a big "pizza" that would feed all who contributed towards it and sometimes more. We would fill the bag up with all the ingredients we wanted in it then fill it with the hot water from the coffee machine. We would then flatten it out at least an inch or so deep and as it cooked it would begin to spread. Once done cooking, we would cut it up and eat it.

I thank God for every meal the prison provided but I must say that the food wasn't too desirable. We were served three meals a day Monday through Friday and only two meals a day on Saturday and Sunday. There were times that I ate food that I wouldn't have never eaten if I had a choice. I thank God for providing for me through fellow inmates from my hometown and others that I had befriended during that time and when I had food and they didn't, I would share mine with them.

I remember one day while I was still in B-Unit, a man from my hometown named Jam wanted me to give him some of my food that I had gotten from the store and I told him no because of the reason he wanted it. He was a gambler and had gambled all that he had and lost it and now wanted to borrow some stuff from me in attempt to win his stuff back or possibly lose mine as well. After telling him no, he was so upset with me and even begin to curse and threaten me. He told me that he was going to send someone up to my room to handle me. From my understanding, he was saying that he was going to send someone to my room to assault me sexually. I can't say I wasn't a little afraid, but I knew it was not the time to show any fear. Instead going in my room and locking myself in and have him and others think I was afraid of them, I stepped inside my room and left the door wide-open and waited for someone to come in. I stood a few feet away from my door and I thought to myself, *"if anyone steps their foot across the threshold to my room I am going to "go off" and punch them in their face as hard as I can and defend myself."* After waiting for a while, no one came. Jam and I reconciled afterward.

The prison had a lot of "Booty Bandits" *(Men who raped other men)* in it and the majority of them was in B-Unit. I remember one day I had sold some Benadryl to a couple of inmates. When I went to get the pay for it, they told me that I could get the Benadryl back but for some reason they wouldn't hand it to me. They told me that it was in their room on the bed. So, I had a decision to make very quickly, either allow them to take my Benadryl and be looked at as someone you can take something from or walk into their room and get it back myself and risk being locked in the room with them to defend my manhood. I was in a lose/lose situation really. The choice I made was the more risky one and probably a bad choice altogether now that I think about it. I chose to walk into their room and get my Benadryl off of their bed. As I walked into their room they stood at the doorway, one on each side. It was only the grace and mercy of God that allowed me to do something like that and walk back out of that room without being touched. I believe those two inmates were known for raping others, they could've easily locked me in the room with them and I would've had to fight for my life literally. There's possibility that I would've never made it back out of that room alive or at least 'untouched'. I had already psyched myself out to believe that if I someone ever tried to sexually assault me, they would have to kill me because I wouldn't have been able to live like that.

◄ SOMETHING TO BE PROUD OF ►

After about three failed attempts, I finally passed the practice GED *(General Education Development)* test. Shortly after that, I took the real GED test and passed it on the first try. The pre-GED test, in my opinion, was much harder than the real test. I was so glad to receive my GED along with a $500 "Hope" voucher, because at least now I had accomplished something in life that I knew my family and I could be proud of. Before I was incarcerated, I was in the ninth grade for the second time before I completely dropped out of high school. I had been expelled from school for a second time and was barely attending *Bibb County's Alternative School* for their "Eighteen-week" program. I believe being in the alternative school hurt me more than it helped me. What do you expect when you put all of the city's at-risk students in one school for months at a time? I was very impressionable as a teenager, so it was easy to influence me to do wrong. Now that I think about it, a large number of the young boys and girls that I went to the alternative school with are in prison right now, have been to prison, or dead. Back then, graduating from high school and going to college were not in my future plans so being able to obtain my GED while I was incarcerated was major to me. It was something to be proud about. And to add to the hype, I received it the same year that I was supposed to have graduated from high school.

I was allowed to begin trade school after I received my GED. At that time, there were numerous trades that we could choose to take including *Basic Automotive Detailing and Maintenance, Culinary Arts, Automotive Mechanics, Body Shop, Electric Repair, Computer Technology*, and more. I chose to take the *Basic Automotive Detailing and Maintenance* course. It was a short course where I learned many things about cars within the six weeks or so that I was taking the class. I completed the course and received a certificate of completion for fifteen hours from *North GA Technical College.*

My mother was still married to Rich and her and my brother was suffering a lot of things from his drug addiction on the outside of the prison walls I was trapped in. I wish I could've been there to help them, but there was no way possible for that to happen. My brother ended up moving in with his friend's family to get away from all the drama. Rich had begun to take things such as my mother's jewelry and my brother's clothes and video games and sell them for drugs. The Bible tells us that we should not be unequally yoked together with unbelievers, but she chose to marry him anyway. Maybe she thought he would change over time, I don't know. It made me so mad to know that all of these things were going on in their life and I couldn't do nothing about it. I was locked away, "out of sight and out of mind". How could I protect them from over 100 miles away stuck behind barbed-wire fences and thick walls?

◄ THE FAITH-BASED DORM ►

James 4:4 (NKJV) "Adulterers and adulteresses! Do you not know that friendship with the world is enmity with God? Whoever therefore wants to be a friend of the world makes himself an enemy of God."

Although I don't believe I really knew God, I use

to mention Him in conversations and write songs that had some references of Him in them. I was still writing and performing ungodly raps around that time as well. I was "straddling the fence" in many areas of my life. One song in particular I wrote around that time was called *"Prison Blues"*. Some of the lyrics were,

"Off in "Alto", we got the prison blues...
my fam, my friends have left me, I have one more thing to lose...
and that's my life, it's dark I need light...
I put my trust in God when I was blind He gave me sight...
*one day reading the Bible (**Psalms 27**), it had a ni**a stuck...*
Say when my mom and dad forsake me God will take me up...
He been here through the thick and thin...
bringing the prison blues to an end and forgiving sins...
I put my trust in Him and now I know I can win...
anything I put my mind to even this sentence of ten (years)...
If you give your life to Him today you won't lose...
you will be free forever, no more prison blues..."

And at another time, I wrote this,

"I should've chose a job but instead I chose to rob...
on this long dark road with a frozen heart...
but my Father God, Lord knew what was right for me...
I don't have to step in the ring because He will fight for me...
that's why I'm on my knees praying every night a week...
asking Him to keep on His guiding light for me...
***JESUS**, I thank ya for dying on the cross...*
You paid the cost to be the boss and found me when I was lost..."

I was still using the word "ni**a" at that time, not really knowing how detrimental using that word was. As you can see, I knew some things about God that could've resulted in me living a different lifestyle than the way I was living. I was lost and didn't know it just like most people in the world today that profess to be Christian and live like the rest of the 'world'. From being raised in a home where **JESUS** was talked about and going to church was important, I thought that as long as I did certain things such as talk the talk, then walking the walk wasn't as important. I believe I really wanted to know the Truth, but I was blinded by the lies of the devil.

I maintained good enough behavior to be transferred from B-Unit after being there for six months. I heard that a new "Faith-based/Religious" dorm was being formed in A-Unit and I wanted to be housed there. It was a laid back, low security dorm and all types of inmates from different religions were welcome to co-exist in this one dorm together. Of course though, inmates who weren't religious at all managed to get accepted into the dorm as well. Honestly, I wanted to be in this dorm because it was low security and more peaceful than other areas of the prison. I only wanted the comfortable benefits that the prison was offering at that time and I wasn't the only one, the dorm was full of inmates just like myself. My roommate was a Muslim and a very nice guy. He prayed about five times a day. We didn't talk much about religion, but we were good associates in the case of being roommates.

One day I was in the "day-room" *(the place where we watched TV)* listening to "DSGB" *(Down South GA Boy)* by a rapper from GA on a portable CD player while sitting at a table. The TV was on as well so I began to look at it as well. I can't remember or not if it was chilly in there that day, but I had pulled my arms inside my shirt and made myself comfortable. I was unaware that it was "count time" *(the time when the officers came around and counted all of the inmates in the prison. The officers counted the prisoners several times a day to ensure everyone was still there and had not escaped).* I was still sitting in the "day-room" when Officer Lady was making her rounds and counting all of the inmates in the dorm.

Shortly after "count time" was cleared, Officer Lady and some other correctional officers came down and put me in handcuffs. I was confused about what was going on and made a fuss about it, but I was still taken to the "hole". I later found out that I had been sent to the "hole" for something that I didn't do, a "C-15" *(a masturbation charge).*

On the "DR", Officer Lady stated that she came in the day room and asked me what I was doing and that I replied, *"What does it look like I'm doing?"* with a smile on my face while looking down at my private area. This was a completely false accusation and I'm not sure why Officer Lady lied on me. A lot of the female officers would allow the inmates to do such things. Some even had illegal relationships with inmates, sexually and non-sexually.

I ended up being found guilty when I went to trial at the court inside the prison. I tried to defend myself and tell my side of the story but no one believed me. I stayed in the "hole" for thirty-six days before I was released. To add to that punishment, I was also banned from the "Faith-based/Religious" dorm. My comfort of being in that dorm was taken because of what happened. Maybe it was all a part of God's plan.

1st John 2:3-6 (NKJV) "...Now by this we know that we know Him, if we keep His commandments. He who says, 'I know Him', and does not keep His commandments, is a liar, and the truth is not in him. But whoever keeps His word, truly the love of God is perfected in him. By this we know that we are in Him. He who says he abides in Him ought himself also to walk just as He walked."

◀ THE ANNEX BUILDING ▶

When I finally came out of the hole I was put in the annex building in A-Unit. The annex building was also a low security, open dorm. Almost a year after the young man was murdered in B-Unit, the GDC began to empty the prison of all the adult prisoners, transferring them to other prisons in groups at a time. Almost weekly inmates were being shipped off to other prisons in the state of GA until the only inmates that were left in "Alto" were the juvenile inmates (sixteen years of age and younger). I knew my day would come and I would be leaving "Alto" sooner or later and I pondered where I would be going, hopefully closer to home.

Although I was over two hours away from home, my mother managed to come visit me a few times over the two years I was there and it meant a lot. It was priceless, but me being transferred somewhere closer to home would be perfect for me. My aunt Linda kept in contact with me as well over the years. Having some type of family support really helped out. Prisons are full of inmates that no longer have the support of family or friends. Over time, the support of family and friends begin to fade away. When an inmate is not receiving visitations, letters, accepted phone calls, or packages from family and friends throughout the years, I believe they begin to fell forgotten.

> *Inmates really need that support, it could keep them going, it could keep them focused, and it could possibly keep them alive.*

Hebrews 13:3 (AMP) **"Remember those who are in prison, as if you were their fellow prisoner..."**

Matthew 25:34-40 (NKJV) **"...Then the King will say to those on His right hand, 'Come, you blessed of My Father, inherit the kingdom prepared for you from the foundation of the world: for I was hungry and you gave Me food; I was thirsty and you gave Me drink; I was a stranger and you took Me in; I was naked and you clothed Me; I was sick and you visited Me; I was in prison and you came to Me...Assuredly, I say to you, inasmuch as you did it to one of these My brethren, you did it to Me'..."**

◀ DOES GOD REALLY LOVE ME? ▶

I believe God was always attempting to get my

attention, but I kept missing the signs. I remember watching *"The Passion of Christ"* movie at a service one day. After seeing **JESUS** die on that cross, I was angry that His own people would condemn Him to be crucified on a cross for no reason. From what I saw on that movie, He didn't do anything worthy of death, but yet He was falsely accused and innocently murdered.

I did not understand wholeheartedly that His death was for a reason and that it was the will of God that He died so that we could live. He was the ultimate sacrifice for sin. I heard a verse quoted from the Bible before about God loving the world so much that He gave His Son and that whoever believed in Him would not perish but they would have everlasting life (**John 3:16**). *"Did God really love me that much that He would send His own Son for me?"*

There were other services we would have other than the regular church services that were held in the Chapel on the weekends. Different ministries and ministers would come in from the "free world" and have services with us during the week as well. I remember going to a service that was held in the school building one evening where some bikers came in and taught us the word of God. They were dressed in their motorcycle gear and all, it was *'cool'*. That night I learned that it was God's desire that I be made the righteousness of God in Christ (**2nd Corinthians 5:21**). I remember writing *"I am..."* in front of *"...the righteousness of God..."* in my Bible.

◀ WEED IN MY POCKET ▶

One day a friend of mine named Harry and I bought a joint of weed together from another inmate. Harry had been my friend since the *Macon RYDC* days and we maintained that friendship in prison.

I had the joint in my pocket and we had planned to smoke it soon after. I was walking through the open dorm and I overheard a conversation that caused to me to stop in my tracks and listen. An older inmate was talking with a few of the younger inmates concerning marijuana being a mind altering drug. I remember listening intently while he spoke to them and what he was saying really grasped me. As I thought back on the day I was arrested, I begin to agree with what he was saying. I believed my addiction to weed was part of what drove me to do the things that I might not have done had I not been high from smoking marijuana or seeking to be high.

Before I knew it, I was reaching in my pocket and handing the joint of weed to Harry and telling him that I was done smoking. That was in December, 2004, I never smoked marijuana another day after that. I give God the glory for that moment. I don't believe it was just by my will power that allowed me to walk away from a marijuana addiction. I was a real addict and I believe that it was the supernatural power of God that graced me to do it. He took the taste out of my mouth and the desire out of my heart for it. This began the process of freedom for me concerning smoking. I was still smoking cigarettes and "Black and Mild" cigars after this, but not for long. The head of the giant (marijuana) had been cut off. I started to pray to God more about helping me to stop smoking. After praying one day, my chest begin to hurt badly after taking puffs of a cigarette and that was it for me. I refused to continue to do something that caused me to hurt like this. The "Black and Mild" cigars were last on the list to go.

It was around this time I ran back into Q who I was in C-Unit with, he was moved to the dorm I was in at the annex building. Q had been a great influence in my life and taught me some things. He was a good man and a great friend to have. He had fallen off of the path of walking with the Lord by time we reconnected. I'm not sure what happened, maybe all the time he had begun to weigh in on him and he just gave up on his faith in God and walking a righteous path. In the annex building, I remember him telling me a dream he had that he believed God had given him, warning him of the outcome of his life if he stayed on the path he was on at that time (which was not the path that leads to life). He said, in the dream he was walking and everything he saw was red, from the ground, the sky, etc. He said he believed he was walking through Hell. I can't remember what I said to give him some kind of encouragement but I hoped that he would get back on the right path.

My nineteenth birthday had just passed and the day finally came that I was transferred from "Alto". It happened in the same month in which I arrived at the prison two years prior, February, 2005. My next dwelling place would be closer to home and at this prison, "Black and Mild" cigars wasn't on the store list at all. God was showing Himself to be faithful to answer my prayers although I was still living a lifestyle that was outside of having a real relationship with him. I was living life the way I thought it should be lived as a Christian.

When I arrived at the new prison, I was given a "detail" *(job to do)*. One day while we were at detail, an inmate from my hometown named 30 (who was in the same dorm as I was in) managed to sneak a "Black and Mild" cigar through security and back into the prison. He offered me some and I smoked a joint of it with him. I remember feeling dizzy and light-headed. After that day, I believe that was my last time smoking altogether. The weed, the cigarettes, and the "Black and Mild" cigars was gone.

*1st Corinthian 6:20 (NKJV) "...**Glorify God in your body and in your spirit, which are God's.**"*

PART 3:

THE BUTTERFLY

10

Raised From the Dead

◄ LIKE LAZARUS ►

Hancock State Prison (located in the middle GA area in the city of Sparta) would be my home for a while. I was housed in the annex building of the prison, not on the main compound. It was a low security area and I was allowed to go outside of the prison to work, for no pay of course.

On February 19th, 2005, I went to a church service that was held in the evening. There was a minister there from the "free world" that came in to share the Word of God with us. Ministers came in all the time, taking time out of their schedules and away from their family to come and have services with us. Going to the church services was not mandatory, but I chose to go. I'd been to innumerous church services and heard the Word preached before, but this day something happened that had never happened before and my whole life was changed.

The minister begin preaching the Word and saying many things, but the main thing I remember is her telling us about Lazarus. I remember hearing her speak about Lazarus and how **JESUS** raised him from the dead and in the midst of her sharing the Word, I had a supernatural encounter with God. I believe with all my heart that God spoke to me! It felt like God himself was grabbing me by my shirt as a loving father would do to his son when he really wanted him to pay attention and listen to something important he was about to say. He was saying that He could do the same for me (as He did for Lazarus). Instantly, it's like a light bulb came on inside of me, I knew exactly what He meant. He meant that He could raise me up from the dead and make me alive in Him. I was dead, I thought I was living, but I was dead and needed to be raised up by **JESUS**. I've heard the Gospel message of **JESUS** Christ and the Word of God many times in my life, but finally my eyes were open to God in a whole new way. God invaded my life and gave me the opportunity to truly repent and ask Him to forgive me of my sins. I earnestly asked Christ to come into my life (my heart); I didn't wait till the altar call, As I was sitting in my seat with tears in my eyes and a soft heart towards the Lord, I cried out to Him and He heard me, forgave me of my sins, and received me as His own; *Hallelujah!!!*

I saw the Lord for who He truly was, the one I needed, and I saw myself for who I truly was, a sinner. At that moment, I knew I needed to be saved and that **JESUS**, the Son of the living God, was the only one who could save me. No one else could do it; I needed Him! My search was over! I was running, but now I was looking at a wall with nowhere to go. Saying yes to God was my only way out.

I believe I really always wanted to live for God before this moment, but the fact that I already believed that I was living for Him kept me blind, bound, and missing out on true relationship with God, which is through His Son, full of His Spirit, and in obedience to His Word.

I don't even remember the minister's name nor did she know that I had been born again right there in the midst of the service because I didn't make an announcement of my conversion, but I believe in Heaven it shall be revealed to her; what a joyous day that will be! I don't remember ever seeing that minister again after that day. I left the cafeteria completely changed, I was brand new! I went in there dead and walked out of there alive. I had been born again, born from above, born of God. God had opened my eyes and raised me from the dead!

> *"Fast forward to the day that I really got saved...*
> *turned on to His mercy and grace...*
> *love and forgiveness was right in my face...*
> *and I got me a taste, yeah, I got me a taste (my eyes open)...*
> *I heard the Gospel preached when I nineteen...*
> *and it struck my heart like lightning...*
> *now I realize God's love for me...*
> *Christ died for me to save me from me...*
> *I knew that I was a sinner and I needed saving...*
> *and I knew that only JESUS Christ could save me...*
> *I realized that I was an enemy to God...*
> *and that I wasn't His friend like I thought I was...*
> *and like Lazarus, only He could raise me...*
> *from the dead, new life is what He gave me...*

John 3:3-8 (NKJV) **"JESUS answered and said to him, 'Most assuredly, I say to you, unless one is born again,** *he cannot see the kingdom of God.' Nicodemus said to Him, 'How can a man be born when he is old? Can he enter a second time into his mother's womb and be born?' JESUS answered, 'Most assuredly, I say to you, unless one is born of water and the Spirit, he cannot enter the kingdom of God. That which is born of the flesh is flesh, and that which is born of the Spirit is spirit. Do not marvel that I said to you, 'You must be born again.' The wind blows where it wishes, and you hear the sound of it, but cannot tell where it comes from and where it goes. So is everyone who is born of the Spirit'..."*

◄ EXPERIENCING CONVICTION ►

When I finally made it back into my dorm things were different. I was immediately convicted of God about the lyrics (rap) I was passionately writing at that time and had been writing since around the age of fourteen or so. All of a sudden I knew that I could not continue to write and rap like that any longer. I remember taking out my folder which was full of lyrics that I had written over the years of my incarceration and began to ball up sheet after sheet until there was a large pile of balled up paper on my bed. Those songs were full of lyrics that I had written that glorified the lifestyle of selling drugs, smoking weed, murder, fornication, gang activity, ungodly neighborhood affiliation, etc. I had been writing and rapping this way for a long time and I saw nothing wrong with it, but on that day I began to see it for what it truly was, poison. I believe I only kept the raps that were positive or had lyrics about God in it, but the rest was thrown away.

I was known as a rapper while I was in "Alto" and I was starting to be known as one at *Hancock State Prison* also, so doing what I did made inmates question what I was doing. I began to read the Bible, pray, and go to church service more than I had ever done my whole incarceration before that time and to my amazement I began to understand some Scriptures. I was attending church services almost daily. I don't believe I had ever understood the Word of God like this before. It was like the words were beginning to come alive and I began to connect with what I was reading. The Holy Spirit inspired Word of God was becoming real to me in ways that I had never experienced before. My mother had written me a letter a while back that contained three Scriptures that I would read often, **Psalms 27**, **Psalms 51**, and **Psalms 91**.

A few weeks after I had stopped rapping, I began to desire to start back doing it again, but not in the manner I was doing it before. This is the moment I believe God was revealing to me that I could still rap, but that there was a better way for me to do it. I began to write lyrics about Him. I rapped about His love, His truth, and how He changed me. I wanted to make Him known. What I had been filling myself up with over those few weeks began to pour out little by little onto the paper I was writing lyrics on. This was all new to me. I wrote these lyrics around that time,

"I know your listening, but answer this question...
would you rather be free and still locked up in sin?...
or locked up in the 'pen' but free within?...
I'm free in the 'pen' ready to hit the streets again...

fresh out of Hancock...
carrying the Word of God, no pistol in my hand cocked..."

I believe people in the dorm began to see a difference in me and I began to make it known here and there.

There was a guy named Bread in the dorm next to me that I knew from the streets and one day while we were out on the yard some of the inmates were taking turns rapping and he asked me to rap an old song that I had written about my hometown. In this particular song he wanted me to rap, I glorified gang activity, murder, and more. I begin telling him no, but he kept on asking me and I eventually compromised and rapped the song for the crowd of inmates and everyone was enjoying it except me. In the midst of rapping the song, I looked up and saw one of my new Christian brothers named James standing a short distance away outside of the crowd I was entertaining and he had a look of disappointment on his face, a look that pricked my heart.

I knew I wasn't supposed to be rapping like that any longer. I felt sorry for giving in to the pressure of being asked continuously to rap the song. His look reminded me of **Matthew 26:57-75**, when **JESUS** was arrested in the Garden of Gethsemane and taken to the house of the high priest, Caiaphas, where he was accused of many things and mistreated. One of His disciples named Peter followed Him as His captors took Him away to be accused and condemned to die.

In the midst of the night, Peter was approached on three separate occasions by witnesses who accused him of being a follower of **JESUS** Christ and all three times he denied their accusations. He had been walking with **JESUS** for three years, but at that moment, he boldly professed three times that he didn't know **JESUS**. On the third time he denied knowing **JESUS**, a rooster crowed and immediately Peter remembered what **JESUS** had told him. Earlier that day, **JESUS** told him that he would deny Him three times before the rooster crowed the next morning. Peter didn't believe he would do such a thing and told Him that he was willing to go with Him and die with Him.

I can imagine how Peter felt after hearing the crow of the rooster and then remembering what **JESUS** had told him. I can imagine he was struck to the core of his being when he realized how he had indeed denied his Lord and friend. The feeling he must've felt at that moment is what I believe I felt when I saw James looking at me while I was in the midst of non-believers glorifying a sinful lifestyle.

Regardless of what people may say, there is a way that God wants us to live. He desires that we live a holy lifestyle before Him and we can only do that submitted to His Word and His Spirit. There are many people in the world today that sing or rap songs that do not glorify God in any way, shape, or form. They live lifestyles that go against the very nature of God and have no conviction of wrong doing. Some of these same people profess that they are of the Christian faith, but according to God's Word, they are only liars (**1ˢᵗ John 1:5-7**). Scripture also says that we should *"walk, even as He walked"* (**1ˢᵗ John 2:6**) and we shouldn't only want to profess with our mouth that we are Christians, we should also want our lifestyle to reflect it as well.

On another occasion, I was in the bathroom alone in a stall where no one could see me. I had went in there to masturbate, not knowing that God would deliver me from masturbation altogether that day. While I was in the bathroom, I looked up and saw a female officer walk by, it was "count time" and I didn't know it. After the count had been cleared, I found out that I had been written up for being out of place during "count time". I was supposed to have been standing by my bed during that time, but instead I was in the bathroom. What did I get out of this? I was convicted of my sin and saw the truth that God was opening my eyes to see that I was in error of the way He desired for me to live. As the loving Father He is, He was showing me right from wrong. He was showing me that masturbation and self-gratification was wrong in His sight. It was sin in His eyes and even though I wasn't caught by an officer for doing it, God saw me and allowed me to be written up. He was correcting me because He wanted me to be clean. JESUS said, if a man looks upon a woman and lusts in his heart after her then he has already committed the act of adultery. When masturbation takes place, lust in the heart takes place also, and that's before, during, and after the act of it.

Matthew 5:27-30 (NKJV) "...But I say to you that whoever looks at a woman to lust for her has already committed adultery with her in his heart...If your right eye causes you to sin, pluck it out and cast it from you...and if your right hand causes you to sin, cut it off and cast it from you; for it is more profitable for you that one of your members perish, than for your whole body to be cast in hell."

◀ TAKING A STAND ▶

My Christian brother, James, was a great guy to be around. One day he posted a letter up on the wall in his dorm requesting that anyone who had questions concerning the Bible or any doubts about the Bible to meet him on the yard so that he could give them an answer to their confusion. Around that time, he was in a place where he was tired of hearing religious and non-religious people speaking against **JESUS**, Christianity, and the inerrant Word of God (the Bible), so he wanted to take a stand for **JESUS** and give them truth for their doubts.

The Warden was walking around the building and went into James' dorm and saw the letter that he had posted on the wall. Afterwards, he called James into the hallway. The Warden told him that he couldn't have a meeting like this. James replied and said, *"We can meet for basketball and other things, but not to share the Word?"* He told the Warden that he would pray about it and would do whatever God told him to do.

The day of the meeting came and a few of the Christian brothers from different dorms met on the yard together. James knew that he would be under surveillance and that he could possibly be sent to the "hole" for meeting after the Warden told him not to, but he saw it more important to obey God above what the

Warden had told him **(Acts 5:29)**. Before coming on the yard he stuck his Bible in the back of his pants where his belt held it in place. Unfortunately, none of the doubters showed up, so we discussed some things and afterwards prayed together. We all got into a circle and linked together hand in hand and began to pray. To my amazement, the prayer circle was broken up by a correctional officer who told us that we couldn't pray in the manner we were doing it. After a few words, James was put in handcuffs and taken to the "hole" and the rest of us were let off with a warning.

Inmates could come together for almost anything, but unfortunately they couldn't come together to hold hands and pray to God collectively.

11

New Life

> "Eyes open, new start...
> He opened me up and gave me a new spirit and a new heart...
> just as He promised by the mouth of His Prophet...
> Ezekiel, right before them dry bones start rising...
> I am so grateful for mercy and compassion...
> His grace is everlasting, saved me when I was crashing...
> Eyes open, He is my God...
> He has given me one way and put His fear in my heart...
> just as He promised by the mouth of His Prophet...
> Jeremiah, after he was locked up by King Zedekiah...
> I am so grateful for the forgiveness of sins...
> and eternal life, I will be getting in...
> not because of my good deeds, nor my religious duties...
> but all by the resurrected Christ, He's so beautiful..."

◄ WALKING FOR MILES ►

Although I was still incarcerated, I started to feel freer. Christ had given me freedom that extended beyond the thick walls of the dorm, the barb-wired fences, and the constant supervision of guards (armed and unarmed). I was what I call a "free inmate" *(incarcerated, but free in Christ)*. I was free indeed! **JESUS** said, *"...If the Son therefore shall make you free, you shall be free indeed."* **(John 8:36)**. God was working in me a desire to really know Him. I found myself reading the Bible, praying, and going to church service more than I had ever done before and this time I began to understand it more and more.

The dorm I was in was so laid back, I don't even remember anyone fighting or anything like that. The majority of the inmates was positive and peaceful from what I remember. I tried my best to mostly surround myself with inmates who I considered at that time to be good guys. Most of them were more positive than they were Christian, nonetheless, they were good company to be around. We played cards, monopoly, exercised, and things of that nature to pass time outside of the daily details we were assigned to do. I spent a lot of time listening to music as well. I stopped listening to rap so much and I begin to listen to more love music (R and B). At that time, I thought it was cleaner and safer than the rap music that I once listened to. Now today, I realize that it's not the genre of music that is the problem, but the belief system of the person on the microphone. With that being said, some R and B songs can be just as poisonous and ungodly as rap some songs because of the content that it can be filled with.

On my detail, we walked for miles cleaning the sidewalks of the roads by picking up trash in Sparta, GA. I also remember doing some work in Gordon, GA, one day at a school. Spring and Summer times are very hot in GA and we would bear the heat of the day almost daily walking for nearly ten miles some days while picking up trash along the way. I remember once asking the officers if I could go on "PC" because I didn't want to continue to go out day after day and walk all those miles in the heat. I told them that I felt like my life was in danger, but my request was denied.

The blessing of being out there however was being able to see other people that were in the "free world". I had been incarcerated for almost three years by that time, so seeing houses, cars riding by, and woman outside of the prison was a bonus for me.

◄ THE VINE AND THE BRANCHES ►

"He was the word of God made flesh...
even though He was God He humbled himself and became less...
***Philippians 2,** read it through...*
I'm praying that the Spirit will open your eyes to something new...
and bring you to your knees in worship to the King...
He is the true vine, to Him we need to cling...
***John 15,** we are only branches...*
and apart from him we can do nothing...
He was crucified, pierced in His side...
blood and water flowed out for His beautiful bride...
He gave up the ghost, hung His head, and died...
surely this was the Son of God..."

One day while we were on the detail walking and picking up trash as usual, I looked up and saw a big tree, it was green and looked healthy. I noticed that in the middle of the tree were broken branches that caused the tree to be brown in that area. Instantly John chapter 15 came to my mind. Scripture says that, *"the Comforter, which is the Holy Spirit, will teach us all things and bring all things to our remembrance whatsoever JESUS has said to us."* **(John 14:26)**. I was blown away by the revelation He was giving me concerning being connected to the true vine, **JESUS** Christ.

All the branches that were properly connected to the tree were still green, healthy, and upright. The tree and the good branches were one. However, the branches in the middle of the tree that had been broken and disconnected from the tree were hanging downwards, their leaves were brown and dry. The strong, healthy branches had life in them because of their union (connection) with the tree, but the broken branches were weak and becoming more and more lifeless because of the disconnection. Their union with the tree had been cut off; the flow of life from the tree to those branches had been stopped. I'm not sure how long those broken branches had been hanging on like that, but I can imagine that at first, even though they had been disconnected from their source of life, they were still green and looked to be prospering as the rest of the unbroken branches. Nevertheless, as day after day went by, they begin to look more and more lifeless due to the separation that had taken place days, weeks, or even months before.

As Christians, it's vital that we stayed connected to our source of life, which is the true vine JESUS. We have to always remember that we are only branches and separated from Him we can do nothing. Apart from Him we will be as those broken branches were, lifeless and withering away. Maybe not at first, but the longer we go separated, the drier and more unfruitful we become. If we stay disconnected, we will eventually become lifeless. When we are connected to Him, we prosper, flourish, and stay full of life; we are green and we bear fruit. If you are in a place right now and you are not connected, then I encourage you to repent now and get reconnected to the source of life, there is grace for you to repair your relationship with God. Scripture says, "He who has the Son has life; he who does not have the Son of God does not have life." (1ˢᵗ John 5:12). JESUS Christ is the true vine! JESUS Christ is the source of life! Stay connected to the vine!

John 15:1-7 (AMP) "I AM the True Vine, and My Father is the Vine dresser. Any branch in Me that does not bear fruit [that stops bearing] He cuts away (trims off, takes away); and He cleanses and repeatedly prunes every branch that continues to bear fruit, to make it bear more and richer and more excellent fruit. You are cleansed and pruned already, because of the word which I have given you [the teachings I have discussed with you]. Dwell in Me, and I will dwell in you. [Live in Me, and I will live in you.] Just as no branch can bear fruit of itself without abiding in (being vitally united to) the vine, neither can you bear fruit unless you abide in Me. I am the Vine; you are the branches. Whoever lives in Me and I in him bears much (abundant) fruit. However, apart from Me [cut off from vital union with Me] you can do nothing. If a person does not dwell in Me, he is thrown out like a [broken-off] branch, and withers; such branches are gathered up and thrown into the fire, and they are burned. If you live in Me [abide vitally united to Me] and My words remain in you and continue to live in your hearts, ask whatever you will, and it shall be done for you."

Spring, 2005...

I remember going to a church service a short while before I went home. The minister of the service told us to write down something that we wanted God to do for us within forty days from that day. At that time, the only greatest thing I wanted from God was to be released from prison. Some may say that my request was a bit much with me still having to serve about seven more months before I was even eligible for parole, but going home is what I wanted.

By that time, I had been incarcerated nearly three full years, so I only had one more year to serve and I would be a free man May, 2006. I knew that if the parole board decided to pardon me, I would be released early as January, 2006, (about four months earlier than I was supposed to), but I wanted to leave much sooner than that.

I had maintained good behavior since being in *Hancock State Prison* and it was looking promising for me to be released on parole when that time came around in January, but I didn't want to wait till then.

Weeks went by and on June 27th an officer came and told me that I would be going home on June 29th. Honestly, I did not believe the officer because I knew my "TPM" *(Tentative Parole Month)* was seven months away in January and the officer was telling me that I was going home in two days. At that point, I can't remember if I even thought about what the minister had us do a short while prior to that day.

The next day my hopes were really high, I was so excited! The other inmates knew I was going home as well so they began to ask me for some of the things I possessed. I remember leaving everything I had with them except my letters, pictures, a folder full of lyrics (raps) I had written, my Bible, and a few other things. I was going home so I no longer needed most of the stuff that I possessed.

◄ GOING HOME A NEW MAN ►

The next morning, I was taken to the front of the prison where I waited for about an hour or so. To my surprise, my mother and my auntie had come to pick me up so I did not have to catch a Greyhound bus home to Macon, GA. I still couldn't believe it.

I was given some brown khaki pants, a white button-down, short-sleeved shirt, and some black and white shoes to wear home. I was also given an "ID" (identification card) with my prison mug-shot, social security number, and some other information on it, and a check for about $35 issued from the *Georgia Department of Corrections.*

An officer walked me to the front of the prison and the gate was opened for me. I was a free man, but I just stood there. After a moment of standing there, the officer said, "You can go." and I proceeded forward. For thirty-seven months I had been told what to do and when to do it. When to eat, when to go to bed, when to wake up, and now I was waiting to be told to go. I walked forward a free man, free indeed! Naturally, I was free from prison and spiritually made free by **JESUS**.

> *"I thank God for giving me grace...*
> *in the midst of doing time I was seeking his face...*
> *I received **JESUS** at the age of nineteen...*
> *I served three years, then I was set free...*
> *Lord, I thank You for what You did for me...*
> *You deserve the honor, the praise, and the glory..."*

◀ THE FREE WORLD ▶

After serving three years, one month, and about six days (1,133 days total), I was released from *Hancock State Prison* at the age of nineteen. I hugged my mother and my auntie before getting into the vehicle that would take me home. I got a little car sick on the ride home because at that time I hadn't ridden in a small vehicle in over three years. We stopped at one my favorite fast-food restaurants on the way home and got something to eat. My mother and brother had moved in with my granny (grandmother) while I was in prison and that's where I resided as well when I came home, back in *Pleasant Hill*.

Upon my release, I had to report to my parole officer the next day. Of course, I was there on time. I stayed on parole for about eleven months and wore an ankle monitor for about four of those months before it was cut off of my leg by my parole officer. While wearing the monitor, I was only allowed to be away from home for twelve hours a day (7am-7pm). The only way I could leave the house earlier or stay away later was if I had a job that required me to do so. I also had to pay fees to my parole officer monthly for being on parole and for wearing the ankle monitor. It was also mandatory that I found a job, work, and do community service.

I applied at a fast-food restaurant and the manager gave me a chance although I was still on parole and wearing a monitor on my ankle. I was hired to work the 2nd shift on which I worked from 3pm-11pm at least five days a week. At that time, we didn't have a car so I walked from Pleasant Hill all the way to where my job was located on Vineville Ave. and back home almost every day I had to work.

I struggled and fell into sin often as a new Christian after coming home from prison. Ultimately, I wanted to please God with my life, but I also wanted to have sex at times. About two weeks after I had come home from prison I fornicated and it left me feeling dirty and far from God although I repented afterward. I wanted to live for God whole heartedly, but I kept getting caught up and giving in to temptation and sometimes intentionally putting myself in certain situations that would end up with me sinning. I'm not condoning anyone to marry for sex, but I understood that sex wasn't the problem, the problem was me having sex with someone who wasn't my wife. Sex amongst a married couple is beautiful in the eyes of the Lord, but sex amongst unmarried couples is called fornication and it is sin in the eyes of God.

God kept the fire burning in my heart for Him and conviction of sin would not leave me alone. I thank God for the forgiveness of sins. God wanted me free from sin. He gave me strength to be bold and maintain my confession of **JESUS** being the Lord of my life in the midst of old friends who stopped by my house to visit me when they heard I had come home from prison. When I ran into old friends and affiliates, I let them know that I was not the same person they once knew. I told them that I wasn't about the street life, drugs, or gang affiliation anymore and I also told them why, **JESUS**. I needed to show them **JESUS** though, not just talk about Him. I continued to pray, read the Bible, go to church, and make efforts to apply the Word of God to my life. I was a new creature and no matter how many times I fell, God gave me the strength to get up and keep pressing towards Him and not go back to living the way I once lived.

I started back going to *"Nu-Sight Ministries"*. It was there that I was given my first opportunity to glorify God through rap. Although I was very nervous, the excitement of being able to praise God in that way kept me going and it blessed the hearers.

> *"I got locked up and met **JESUS**...*
> *but He wasn't doing time He was doing fine...*
> *and I was going down, I almost drowned...*
> *but He's a lifeguard, certified to save lives...*
> *and He saved mine, yes He changed mines...*
> *gave me a new look, He rearranged mine...*
> ***JESUS** is the way, salvation in no other...*
> *at the name of **JESUS** all knees will buckle...*
> *bow down and all tongues confess...*
> *that **JESUS** is Lord, to the glory of God..."*

While in prison, I prayed to God and asked Him to give me a wife and He was faithful to answer my prayers. He gave me His best, my wife, Sunshine. We began dating October 17th, 2005. When I first met my wife, she was not a Christian, but she did attend church. After we began dating, she realized that being a Christian was more than just going to church on Sundays and made a decision to get saved for real. We were not wise while we were dating and a few times we ended up in places alone that we shouldn't have been in and in some of those times we ended up giving in to our fleshly desires. At that time, she didn't know anything about the conviction of God I was experiencing. Aside from that she felt as if she had led me the wrong way. It wasn't her fault though, I should have obeyed what I knew to be true, the Word of God, but we had no solid boundaries set in place to avoid fornication at that time.

The "Highway of Compromise" is often traveled by Christians. It is so easy to travel when we are not focused on honoring God daily in all we do, including our conversations and thoughts.

I decided to ask her to marry me and she said yes! We finally moved out of my granny's house and into a nice, big house right off of Houston Ave. in south Macon. Although we were not married yet, we were already living together. My mother allowed Sunshine to stay with us because she felt she had nowhere else to go after her and her Grandmother had fallen out, plus I was making a big fuss about it because she was my girlfriend and soon-to-be wife and I didn't see anything wrong with it at that time.

Around New Year's Day (2006), we agreed to not have sex anymore until we were married. I loved her and I just wanted to please God, so I had gotten to a point in my life that either we were going to get married or split up because I didn't want to continue living that way before God. There is a scripture in the Bible that says, *"It is better to marry than to burn"* (**1ˢᵗ Corinthians 7:9**). My understanding of this scripture was simply how it is written. I thought when it talked about burning, it was talking about burning in Hell's fire. So for me, it was either get married or keep fornicating and go to Hell. I definitely didn't want to go there. **JESUS** didn't save me so that I could die in sin and go to Hell (where He saved me from to begin with). I understand now that when the Scripture spoke of 'burning', it wasn't speaking of Hell, but (to unmarried Christians) 'burning with passion' to have sex and not being able to fulfill the strong desire to do so because of their desire to please God. Scripture also says, *"...To avoid fornication, let every man have his own wife, and let every woman have her own husband"* (**1ˢᵗ Corinthians 7:2**).

We were young in age and young in the faith (of the Lord **JESUS** Christ), but that could not be our *"cloak"* (justification) to continue to fall in that area. We needed to take heed to the Word of God, that would be the only way to keep our way clean (Psalms 119:9).

After dating for about three months, we got married January 28th, 2006, as teenagers (eighteen and nineteen years old). We had a beautiful wedding ceremony at *"Nu-Sight Ministries"*, it was officiated by our Pastor at that time. Our colors were pink and cream. The church was almost full, family and friends came out to witness this wonderful moment in our life. We didn't know what we were doing and probably wasn't even ready to be married, but we loved each other and wanted to be in the will of God.

God gave us our first child that same year, October 26th. We had a few miscarriages before my wife finally conceived. We prayed and believed God that He was able to deliver to us our heart's desire at that moment, and He did. She was truly a miracle from the Lord. God gave us another daughter January 23rd, 2008, and a son February 13th, 2012.

Although I'm ending my story on a good note, everything was not *"Happily Ever After"* after we got married and one day we may write a book about our experiences as a young married couple that will bless many couples around the world, young and old. We went through a great deal of trial and error. Our relationship was very unhealthy for a long time and we are still striving to become one as God meant for us to be. We almost gave up several times and often contemplated getting divorced. I remember one day we actually had divorce papers sitting around in the apartment we were staying in. They were already signed by the both of us, but as days went by, I thought on things and prayed, and I said to the Lord, "You hate divorce, I hate it too..." **(Malachi 2:16)**. I went outside lit our little bar-b-que grill up and burned the divorce papers. Since then, we still have had moments that we wanted to split up, and even had the divorce papers again, but we found ourselves working things out and reconciling time after time. *It was the grace of God at work, we were tired. In this relationship, I am quick to put the finger at my wife, when I am the one that need to be fixed. God desires to show me my mess ups and make me better as an individual, not just my wife. I was focusing on her so much that I couldn't see the part that I played in us falling apart.*

We renewed our vows on my twenty-ninth birthday (January 31st, 2015), after being married for nine years. This time the ceremony was at our new church home *"Lion's Roar Church of JESUS"* and officiated by our Apostles who have been married for over thirty-five years and have poured into our lives tremendously through their support, care, prayers, faith, time, example, and counseling concerning our marriage since the year 2007. They saw us at our worst and were not willing to let us give up although we had already *"threw in the towel"*. They believed in us more than we believed in ourselves and were proud to see us overcoming our troubled past and renewing our vows. Marriage is WORK, but we want God to be glorified in ours.

I have grown so much as a Christian, but I still have a long way to go. I praise God for the growth and for keeping me in His hands. I truly want to be kept and want my life to please Him. I am His and I need Him daily! I have been born again and filled with His Spirit!!! I am in Christ and I am a new creature, old things are passed away and now all things are new. **JESUS** gave me the power to become a son of God and there is no greater feeling in this world than knowing that I belong to Him and He calls me son.

John 1:12 (AMP) *"But to as many as did receive and welcome Him, he gave the right [the authority, the privilege] to become the children of God, that is, to those who believe in (adhere to, trust in, and rely on) His name..."*

2nd Corinthians 5:17-18 (NKJV) *"Therefore, if anyone is in Christ, he is a new creation; old things have passed away; behold, all things have become new. Now all things are of God..."*

Wedding ceremony,
January 28th, 2006.

Wedding vow renewal,
January 31st, 2015.

Our children, January 31st, 2015.

12

We Will All Stand Before Him

*If you have a Bible,
please open it up and read the scriptures that I share.

◄ THE ONLY ONE WE SHOULD FEAR ►

As I look back and think about the day I stood before the judge facing those heavyweight charges, I also think about the day that I will have to stand before the judgment seat of Christ. Truth is, all of mankind will have to stand before the 'Judge of Heaven' one day. You see, I was so afraid standing before the judge at the age of sixteen with charges against me that could've resulted in me spending decades behind bars. I was facing the judge with more than one count of the *"Georgia's Seven Deadly Sins"* crimes.

There I was standing before 'His Honor' with three counts of armed robbery (with a firearm) and one count of kidnapping. I knew there was absolutely no possibility of me going home at that point, however, I did have hope that I wouldn't get so much time to serve. It was like the judge held my entire life in his hands. At his word I could be released immediately and also at his word I could be sent to prison until the day I died, he was in control. Although my lawyer and the DA agreed on dropping all four of my charges to one lesser charge (robbery by force) because I didn't possess a gun during the robberies, the final say was still in the hands of the judge, he had to agree with what they agreed upon or else I was doomed. If he would've declined their agreement, there would've been no one there to rescue me from his fair judgment of a young criminal who purposely went out and committed crimes time after time. Scripture says that we will all have to stand before the judgment seat of Christ to give account unto Him one day (**2nd Corinthians 5:9-11**). We will all answer to Him!

I think about what that day will be like when we stand before the judgment seat of the sinless Son of God whom God the Father gave all judgment to (**John 5:22**). Whatever **JESUS** says, His Father will approve of it. The Apostle, John, said that he saw the resurrected Christ and after seeing Him he fell on his face as if he had suddenly died. John went on to say that **JESUS** had eyes like a flame of fire (**Revelation 1:14-18**) and that the earth and sky fled away from His face (**Revelation 20:11**). I can imagine the fear and awe that must have gripped his heart upon seeing and laying before the Almighty Lord God. If I feared the earthly judge who could only throw me in prison for the rest of my life or even at the worst give me the death penalty, how much more should I fear the 'Judge of the living and the dead'?

For a moment, imagine yourself standing before God unforgiven with multiple charges (sins) knowing that you are guilty and that He has the power to cast you into Hell or either allow you to enter into Heaven according to your works that were never washed in the blood of **JESUS**. What do you think the judgment will be? **JESUS** warned us not to fear man (who can kill the body only and after that do nothing more to us) and He encouraged us to fear God (who has the power to not only kill the body, but also cast the soul into Hell). There will be no paroling out of Hell, no early release, no bail nor bond, or any hope of ever getting out. Please, I beg you, don't allow the devil to deceive you (or you deceive yourself) into believing that you can get into Heaven because you are a good person. Following **JESUS** is the only way into Heaven. We must all be aware how we live in this life, understanding that one day we shall face God and He is just, fair, holy, righteous, and hates sin. He is not bias with His Word, He requires that everyone repent of their sins and trust in His Son **JESUS** Christ.

The only way we can be right with God is through a right relationship with His Son **JESUS**, who gave Himself for us (**1ˢᵗ John 3:16, John 15:13-14, Galatians 1:3-5, Galatians 2:20, Titus 2:11-14**). (**JESUS really gave Himself for us, just meditate on that statement for a while**). That alone is enough for us to honor Him daily. Christ died for the sins of sins of mankind, not so that we could continue living in sin, but so that we could be free from sin and live a life alive unto God that is acceptable in His eyes. **JESUS** is our only hope! Only through Him can we receive true salvation (**Acts 4:12**). Only He can save to the uttermost (**Hebrews 7:25**). Only by His blood can we be saved from the wrath of God (**Romans 5:9**). He is the way, the truth, the life, the only way to God, and the only way to Heaven (**John 14:6**). Only He can fill the void in our life. Only He can give rest to the weary soul (**Matthew 11:28-30**). He has power to allow us to enter into Heaven or cast us into Hell. Denying Christ is like spitting in God's face. God gave His Son because He loved us and desired to have fellowship with us. God was in Christ reconciling the world unto Himself (**2nd Corinthians 5:19**). He knew that we couldn't live the life He desires for us to live on our own and because of the "fall of man" we needed to be redeemed and brought back into fellowship with Himself.

Now, knowing that there will be a judgment day for all mankind, how should we live our lives before He who sees all, knows all, and is soon to return in righteousness to Judge all nations (**Matthew 25:31-33**)? God loves us and has made a way for us to be with Him forever and it's through **JESUS**.

Luke 12:4-5 (NKJV) "...I say to you, My friends, do not be afraid of those who kill the body, and after that have no more that they can do. But I will show you whom you should fear: Fear Him who, after He has killed, has power to cast into hell; yes, I say to you, fear Him!"

◄ GRACE IS NOT A LICENSE FOR SLOPPY LIVING ►

Hallelujah! Praise God for His grace, but 'the grace of God' is not a license that gives us freedom to live a sloppy sinful lifestyle before Him. We must be obedient to Him, obedient to His Word. In fact, the right understanding of grace should fuel us to want to please God more and not the opposite. A desire to know

Him, grow in Him, and "be holy as He is holy" should be ever present within us. I believe there are many people who misuse grace, some ignorantly, and some knowingly. I also believe there are many who teach or preach 'the grace of God' message in such a way that the listeners of it feel free to live lifestyles that does not display Christ and His way. In the book of Titus, Paul had a different revelation of the grace of God and what it should produce. Inspired by the Holy Ghost, he said that *"...the grace of God that brings salvation has appeared to all men, teaching us that, denying ungodliness and worldly lusts, we should live soberly, righteously, and godly in the present age, looking for the blessed hope and glorious appearing of our great God and Savior JESUS Christ, who gave Himself for us, that He might redeem us from every lawless deed and purify for Himself His own special people, zealous for good works..."* (**Titus 2:11-14**). This doesn't sound like the grace message that's being heard the most in our day and time, does it?

He said that 'the grace of God' teaches us to live right before God, denying ungodliness and worldly lusts in the present age (right now in this life), looking for the appearing (return) of Christ. Christ is coming back for His bride (all those that belong to Him, the church, [the people, not the building]). I guarantee you if I told you that a president or a king was coming to visit your home you would have your house clean and in order and even if he delayed, you would still keep everything nice and neat until he showed up, right? **JESUS** is truly coming back for those that believe in Him and how much more should we have our houses (lives) in order for the 'King of kings' who *"gave himself for us"*?

Paul also told Titus to *let no one disregard or despise him* (concerning 'the grace of God', what it truly is, and the lifestyle it truly produces), *but to conduct himself and his teaching so as to demand respect...* **(Titus 2:15 - AMP)**. Please understand what I'm trying to say, I am by no means speaking concerning baby Christians or those that struggle and fall into sin at times, but yet repent and press on following JESUS. I'm speaking concerning those that boldly profess that they are saved and are not convicted to live the life that displays true change. Scripture says that all have come short of the glory of God, and as long as we are in this human flesh, we may continue to come short at times, but that shouldn't stop our pursuit to be holy as He is holy. God is requiring us to live holy before Him **(1st Peter 1:15-16)**, and how can we do that? Through trusting **JESUS**, the power of the Holy Ghost, the knowledge of who God is, and the fear of God. God loves us and He proves it daily, but His love is not in question, ours is. **JESUS** said if someone really loves Him, they would keep His commands **(John 14:15-24)**. So, is it possible to simply say that we love God and not show it? Would our love still be true? Absolutely not. Our tree of *"I love you"* must bear good fruit on it. Our love must be visible, other than that we are the ones that God was speaking about when He spoke through His Prophet, Isaiah, and said, *"These people draw near to Me with their mouth, and honor Me with their lips, but their heart is far from Me. And in vain do they worship*

Me, teaching as doctrines the commandments of men." (**Matthew 15:8-9**). I don't know about you, but I don't want to live like that. **JESUS** said, *"You shall love the Lord your God with all your heart, with all your soul, with all your strength, and with all your mind, and your neighbor as yourself."* (**Mark 12:29-31**).

A right relationship with God and mankind will get us into the Kingdom of Heaven. We can scream to the top of our lungs about how justified we are, sanctified we are, glorified we are, and holy we are, but if our lifestyle doesn't reflect our confession, it doesn't hold any weight in this life nor the next. Let's not continue to abuse the grace of God, but appreciate His grace and allow it to be the reason that we, by His grace, live a lifestyle that is pleasing before Him. We have to purify ourselves, even as He is pure (**1st John 3:3**). God forbid that we willingly continue living our lives in sin believing that grace will take care of everything. We must repent and live the way He desires for us to live. It's not enough to have faith, we must add works to our faith. *"Faith without works is dead"* according to **James (2:26)**.

Romans 6:1-2, 12-13 (NKJV) "...Shall we continue in sin, that grace may abound? God forbid. How shall we, that are dead to sin, live any longer therein?...Let not sin therefore reign in your mortal body, that ye should obey it in the lusts thereof. Neither yield ye your members as instruments of unrighteousness unto sin: but yield yourselves unto God, as those that are alive from the dead, and your members as instruments of righteousness unto God..."

Only those whose names are in the Lamb's book of life will make it into Heaven and those whose names are not found in the book of life will be cast into the lake of fire **(Revelation 20:15)**. It's not in how much power and respect we have. It's not in how much money we possess. It's not in how much tithe and offerings we give. It's not in how many cars and houses we own. It's not in how many gifts and talents we have. It's not in how many different places we've traveled to minister. It's not in how much praise we receive from people or how many people like us. It's not in how big our church or ministry is. It's not in how many members or followers we have. It's not in how many lost souls we've won to Christ. It's not in how successful we are. It's not in what our title is. It's not in how many "likes" or views have on social media. It's not in how many bible verses we've memorized. It's not in how many spiritual songs we know how to sing. It's not in how much of a good person we believe we are. It's not in all of the good things we do. None of this stuff will be the reason why we are able to enter into Heaven.

JESUS said only those that do the will of His Father shall enter into the Kingdom of Heaven **(Matthew 7:21)**. It's only by us being in right relationship with the one true God by receiving and believing on His Son and our name being written in the Lamb's book of life that one will be able to enter in.

JESUS told His followers to not even rejoice that the evil spirits were subject to them. He told them to only rejoice that their names are recorded in Heaven **(Luke 10:20)**. Regardless of what people in the world (Christian and non-Christian alike) are doing and saying, the Bible paints a solid picture of what a born again believer in Christ looks like and how they live their lives according to His way.

Contrary to popular belief, I believe that it's possible for names to be taken out of the Lamb's book of life according to **Revelation 3:5**. Christ Himself spoke to John and told him to write these words down and send it to the church in Sardis, *"...he that overcomes, the same shall be clothed in white clothing, And I will not blot out his name out of the book of life, but I will confess his name before My Father, and before His angels."* After hearing that He will not blot out the names of those that overcome, this question comes to mind, "What about those that don't overcome?" He also said they that overcome will be clothed in white clothing (undefiled garments), not dirty clothing as mentioned in **Revelation 3:4**.

John also mentioned in **Revelation 22:19** about God taking away a person's part out of the book of life for taking away from the words of the prophecy that Christ shared. We have to live a life that is pleasing to Him and strive to obey Him until we see Him. If we miss the mark (mess up, sin) we must repent, turn away from our sin, and keep following **JESUS**.

Paul said that if we are in Christ, we are new creatures (a brand new creation), and that old things are passed away **(2nd Corinthians 5:17-18)**. **JESUS** Christ's blood was shed for the remission (forgiveness) of sins (**Matthew 26:27-28**). We also have redemption through His blood and the door has been opened that we can come to God and confess our sins and ask Him for forgiveness and it will be given to us (**Colossians 1:13-14**). He is faithful and just to forgive us of our sins and cleanse us from all unrighteousness (**1st John 1:8-10**). We must also forgive others as He has forgiven us. **JESUS** said *"...if you forgive men their trespasses, your heavenly Father will also forgive you. But if you do not forgive men their trespasses, neither will your Father forgive your trespasses..."* (**Matthew 6:14-15**). If we don't forgive others for sinning against us, then God won't forgive us for sinning against Him. If we are not forgiven, then we won't be right (at peace) with God.

I had to forgive my dad for not being in my life when I was a young boy and since being released from prison, God has restored our relationship over the years. We have to continually practice walking in forgiveness all the time. In this life, people are going to hurt, offend, and disappoint us at times, but we must choose to forgive them and allow God to heal us of the hurts. He can and will show us how to be free.

◄ SCRIPTURES ON GIVING ACCOUNT TO HIM ►

Revelation 20:11-15 (KJV) "**...I saw a great white throne, and him that sat on it, from whose face the earth and the heaven fled away; and there was found no place for them. And I saw the dead, small and great, stand before God; and the books were opened: and another book was opened, which is the book of life: and the dead were** *judged out of those things which were written in the books, according to their works. And the sea gave up the dead which were in it; and death and hell delivered up the dead which were in them: and they were judged every man according to their works. And death and hell were cast into the lake of fire. This is the second death. And whosoever was not found written in the book of life was cast into the lake of fire."*

Romans 14:10-12 (NKJV) "...We shall all stand before the judgment seat of Christ. For it is written: 'As I live, says the Lord, Every knee shall bow to Me, and every tongue shall confess to God.' So then each of us shall give account of himself to God."

Hebrews 4:13 (NKJV) "...There is no creature hidden from His sight, but all things are naked and open to the eyes of Him to whom we must give account."

1st Peter 1:13-19 (NKJV) "...Therefore gird up the loins of your mind, be sober, and rest your hope fully upon the grace that is to be brought to you at the revelation of JESUS Christ; as obedient children, not conforming yourselves to the former lusts, as in your ignorance; but as He who called you is holy, you also be holy in all your conduct, because it is written, "Be holy, for I am holy." And if you call on the Father, who without partiality judges according to each one's work, conduct yourselves throughout the time of your stay here in fear; knowing that you were not redeemed with corruptible things, like silver or gold, from your aimless conduct received by tradition from your fathers, but with the precious blood of Christ, as of a lamb without blemish and without spot..."

Hebrews 9:26-27 (NKJV) "...He has appeared to put away sin by the sacrifice of Himself. And as it is appointed for men to die once, but after this the judgment..."

2nd Corinthians 5:9-11 (NKJV) "...We make it our aim, whether present or absent, to be well pleasing to Him. For we must all appear before the judgment seat of Christ, that each one may receive the things done in the body, according to what he has done, whether good or bad. Knowing, therefore, the terror of the Lord, we persuade men..."

John 5:22-27 (NKJV) "...The Father judges no one, but has committed all judgment to the Son, that all should honor the Son just as they honor the Father. He who does not honor the Son does not honor the Father who sent Him...He has granted the Son to have life in Himself, and has given Him authority to execute judgment also, because He is the Son of Man..."

Matthew 12:36 (NKJV) "...I say to you that for every idle word men may speak, they will give account of it in the Day of Judgment."

I want to be ready!!!

John 8:31-32, 36 (NKJV) *"...If you abide in My word, you are my disciples indeed. And you shall know the truth, and the truth shall make you free...Therefore if the Son makes you free, you shall be free indeed."*

Psalms 119:9-11 (NKJV) *"...How can a young man cleanse his way? By taking heed according to Your word. With my whole heart I have sought You; Oh, let me not wander from Your commandments! Your word I have hidden in my heart, that I might not sin against You."*

*"...He made me alive, I was dead in trespasses and sins, in which I once walked according to the course of this world, according to the prince of the power of the air, the spirit who now works in the sons of disobedience, among whom also I once conducted myself in the lusts of my flesh, fulfilling the desires of my flesh and of my mind, and were by nature a child of wrath, just as the others. But God, who is rich in mercy, because of His great love with which He loved me, even when I was dead in trespasses, made me alive with Christ (by grace I have been saved), and raised me up, and made me sit in the heavenly places in Christ **JESUS**, that in the ages to come He might show the exceeding riches of His grace in His kindness toward me in Christ **JESUS**. For by grace I have been saved through faith, and that not of myself; it is the gift of God, not of works, lest I should boast. For I am His workmanship, created in Christ **JESUS** for good works, which God prepared beforehand that I should walk in them...Therefore, I am in Christ, I am a new creation; old things have passed away; behold, all things have become new. Now all things are of God, who has reconciled me to Himself through **JESUS** Christ, and has given me the ministry of reconciliation, that is, that God was in Christ reconciling the world to Himself, not imputing their trespasses to them, and has committed to me the word of reconciliation. Now then, I am an ambassador for Christ, as though God were pleading through me: I implore you on Christ's behalf, be reconciled to God. For He made Him who knew no sin to be sin for me, that I might become the righteousness of God in Him...He was slain, and have redeemed me to God by His blood out of every tribe and tongue and people and nation, and have made me a king and a priest to my God; and I shall reign on earth..."* **Ephesians 2:1-10, 2nd Corinthians 5:17-21, Revelation 5:9-10 (NKJV)**, *paraphrased and directed towards myself)*

PRAYER

*Father, I want to know You. I see now more than ever the deep need I have to be in right relationship with You through Your Son **JESUS**. You sent Him because You loved me. I really need you. I know I have been running from you but now I come to You trusting that you will forgive me of my many sins and receive me. I ask that you forgive me, I repent. Clean me God and make me new. Give me a fresh start. My heart is open to You God. Please fill me with Your Holy Spirit and help me to live my life in a way that makes You smile. I don't want to be lost anymore and I thank You that I don't have to be any longer. I thank You for sending **JESUS**. I believe that He died upon a cross for my sins and that He was raised up for my justification. I believe in **JESUS** Christ, I believe that He is alive. I believe that **JESUS** is Lord and the only way to Heaven. Lord, fill my heart with Your love and Your Word. Help me to forgive others who have done me wrong. Show me what to do. Lead me in your way. I want to love you more than anything in this life. I want to see your face. As a sponge soaks and holds in water, let my heart soak and hold in Your Word. Not only do I want to know your Word, I also want to live Your Word. Teach me Your ways. Give me revelation of who **JESUS** is and the strength to follow Him. Fill me with your fire and the fear of the Lord. Help me to obey You. God, Thank you for opening my eyes. Thank you Father for saving my life... Amen!*

*If you prayed this prayer with sincerity, I believe with all my heart that God heard you from wherever you are and have just saved you! I believe your name has just been written in the Lamb's book of life. I believe that He has forgiven you of all your sins and washed you clean. Welcome to the family of God! The angels in Heaven are rejoicing **(Luke 15:10)**. I encourage you to devote yourself to knowing God. Read God's word (The Holy Bible) and pray unto your Father which is in Heaven every day. Ask God to lead you to a solid church in your area. Serve God faithfully.*

*I would love to hear from you and walk with you on this new journey you have embarked upon! Email me at **irepdaking@yahoo.com** to stay connected with me.*

ABOUT THE AUTHOR

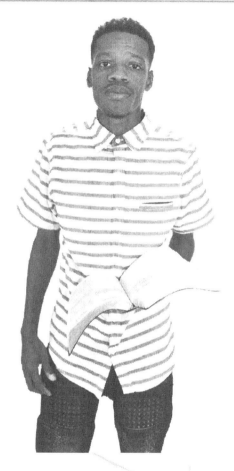

...Since I have been released from prison, God has opened numerous doors of opportunity for me to share my testimony and minister through rap, teaching, and preaching about God's truth, love, forgiveness, return, and soon coming judgment to others and is still opening doors for me to travel and proclaim the Gospel locally and in other areas. I am proof that God can take someone and transform their life no matter how far off the trail

they have wandered. I still reside in Macon, GA, with my wife and children where I am connected to the body of Christ at "Bold as a Lion Family Worship Center" under the leadership of Drs. (Apostles): Carlton and Denise Walker. **JESUS** *Christ is my life and Lord, He has been so faithful to me and it is my greatest desire and prayer that He will be glorified in my life forevermore. I am confident in this one thing, that He who begun a good work in me will complete it...* **(Philippians 1:6)**.

◄ CONTACT INFO ►

iRepDaKING.com
Email: irepdaking@yahoo.com

Psalms of Michael - Vol. 1 (Book)

Born Again (CD)

All Things New (CD)

Made in the USA
Columbia, SC
16 July 2017